TRANSFORMATIONAL
LIVING

TRANSFORMATIONAL
LIVING

Positivity, Mindset, and Persistence

EARL NIGHTINGALE

Published and Distributed by

SOUND WISDOM
PO Box 310
Shippensburg, PA 17257-0310
717-530-2122

info@soundwisdom.com

www.soundwisdom.com

Originally part of Nightingale Success program.

Cover design by Eileen Rockwell

ISBN 13 TP: 978-1-64095-086-3

ISBN 13 eBook: 978-1-64095-087-0

For Worldwide Distribution, Printed in the U.S.A.

1 2 3 4 5 6 / 21 20 19

We are the creators of our own surroundings.

EARL NIGHTINGALE

TABLE OF CONTENTS

PREFACE

ONE OF THE MOST WELL-KNOWN radio broadcasters of all time, Earl Nightingale dedicated his life to sharing his time-tested success strategies. For Nightingale, the most crucial element that determined a person's ability to become successful—emotionally, relationally, and financially—is not the family into which he or she was born or a degree from a top-ranked school; neither is it "good luck" or a person's financial or interpersonal savvy. Rather, it is a person's mindset—his or her perspective on successes and failures, unbreakable optimism, and genuine enjoyment of life—that separates the truly wealthy individuals from the impoverished ones. Indeed, according to Nightingale, not only will the right outlook help you build monetary wealth; it will also enable you to attain what he viewed as the highest form of success—self-actualization: being a psychologically whole, fully functioning, thriving individual with no cognitive dissonance and no reason to let life's many stressors diminish your joy.

Nightingale believed that no matter your circumstances, the right mental framing guarantees your ultimate freedom. All it takes is enthusiasm—a zest for living—and faith in your journey for you to be in control of your situation and to be untarnished by missteps or unfortunate events. As he details in the messages contained in this volume, enthusiasm can easily be cultivated through a number of means: learning, daydreaming, maintaining healthy relationships, and continually pursuing a goal. Like he notes, "Success, as far as a person is concerned, does not lie in achievement. It lies in striving, reaching, attempting." In other words, satisfaction in life can be found by an openness toward the journey—locating and appreciating the wonder in each step it involves.

Transformational Living derives from *The Essence of Success*, a collection of over one hundred of Nightingale's original audio scripts published in 1993 by Nightingale-Conant Corporation. As W. Clement Stone notes in his original foreword, these scripts "have been extracted from the firm's archives and gathered from the private collections of many individuals who have contributed rare tapes and transcriptions to this tribute to one of the great motivational speakers and writers of this century."

Stone further explains: "Nightingale's radio colleague, Stephen D. King, whom Nightingale-Conant selected to narrate the audio version of *The Essence of Success*, recalls that the project began as a simple, heartfelt memorial to a broadcasting great, whose career spanned more than four decades. 'Earl's friends and colleagues began assembling a cross-section of his 40-year output. They took snippets of his tapes, found transcriptions of his early broadcasts, and delved into several hours of never-before-heard tapes of interviews he gave. Soon the project took on a life of its own,' King recalled. 'The more they collected, the more they wanted to collect. Radio old-timers, hearing about the project, contributed rare tapes and transcriptions.' What they assembled has gone on to become far more than a memorial."

Now, those messages in *The Essence of Success* pertaining to cultivating a success mindset have been edited and re-collected in this life-changing volume. The chapters selected will help you overhaul your current way of thinking so that you can go from "surviving" to living exuberantly. If you are not reaping the enjoyment you should be from each day; if you find yourself overcome by worry, fear, or doubt; or if your self-image or outlook is holding you back from attaining your goals, *Transformational Living* will provide you with the concrete tools you need to reframe your perspective and derive more joy out of life.

One of the allegories in this volume captures the power of one's mindset to determine how he or she experiences and engages with the world. Stone writes: "One of my favorite Earl Nightingale recordings is his account of Carl Sandburg's story about the Kansas farmer (Earl called him a 'sodbuster') who, as he contemplated the great mysteries of life, was asked by a passing stranger in a covered wagon, 'What kind of people live around here?' to which the farmer replied, 'Well, stranger, what kind of folks were there in the country you come from?'

"'Well, there was a mostly low-down, lying, thieving, gossiping, backbiting lot of people,' said the stranger. And the farmer replied, 'Well, stranger, I guess that's about the kind of folks you'll find around here.'

"The first wagon was hardly out of sight when another newcomer interrupted the farmer's reverie with the same question: 'What kind of folks was there in the country you came from?' the farmer asked again. 'Well,' said the stranger, 'there was mostly a decent, hard-working, law-abiding, friendly lot of people.' And again the farmer replied, 'Well, I guess, stranger, that's about the kind of folks you'll find around here.'

"In Nightingale's own inimitable way, he tells us that the reality we experience will be that of our own creation. 'Our individual worlds,' he said, 'will respond to us in the way in which we see them. They will become for us that which we expect of them. We are the creators of our own surroundings.'"

As you read the broadcasts in this collection, you'll rediscover the love of life that so many of us lose in adulthood. The luster will return, and you'll never again underestimate the power of curiosity, positivity, and gratitude.

Chapter One

How to Develop a
Winning Attitude

Two Keys to Enthusiasm

READING BERNARD LEVIN'S EXCELLENT PIECE "In Praise of Exuberance," I became concerned anew, as he has, about the general disappearance of exuberance and enthusiasm in the modern world.

It reminded me again of the powerful cartoon I saw some years back by the European artist Fernando Krahn. In the first panel, he shows a group of small schoolchildren entering a street-level subway station. As the children head down to the subway, they're the picture of exuberant joy. They're laughing, playing, and tossing hats in the air, as children do. But in the next panel, we see a group of middle-aged adults coming out of the subway station. They wear the facial expressions of zombies. Their faces display dullness, tedium, and a complete lack of interest or enthusiasm.

There is no caption on the drawing, nor is one needed. The question screams out: "What happened to these people in the years since childhood that has removed every vestige of their zest for life?" In a world filled with wonder and the opportunity for growth and exploration of options, these adults, so representative of big-city crowds—and small-town people, too—have apparently lost every vestige of interest. They are in neutral—in a kind of modern limbo we might characterize as "survival." What happened?

Is it a matter of responsibility? A factor of competition for survival? There's no easy answer, that's for sure. To tell someone he or she should be more enthusiastic is meaningless unless at the same time stimulating triggers of enthusiasm are brought into the picture.

The saddest days of our lives are those days in which we can find nothing to be enthusiastic about. I think you can say that a person's enthusiasm is in direct proportion to the importance of what it is he's looking forward to. Thus, there are all sorts of degrees of enthusiasm. People tend to be mildly enthusiastic on Friday simply because it's the last day of the week and they've got a free weekend coming up. People tend to be more enthusiastic about going home after work at night than they are about leaving for work in the morning. But the most fortunate people on earth are those who live most of their lives in a state of energizing enthusiasm.

And do you know what the key to enthusiasm is? Well, there are two keys, really. One comes from learning. The other comes from accomplishment. Learning new things tends to keep our enthusiasm high. Perhaps this explains the natural enthusiasm of the children depicted in Krahn's cartoon. They're naturally enthusiastic, and they're naturally happy. The reason adults tend to lose a lot of their enthusiasm for living is that they usually stop learning.

As soon as school's over, they take the position, consciously or unconsciously, that they know enough. Any learning they do from that point on they do passively through the natural passage of time and experience—or again, passively through the media, newspapers, radio, or television. If new learning comes to them, it does so largely through no effort or at least minimal effort on their part.

Learning little that is new or interesting, their lives become repetitious and settle down into well-worn grooves. They see the same people and go through the same motions every day, and gradually or quickly all or most of their enthusiasm fades from their lives.

The second key usually ties in with the first, the second key being accomplishment. It's really hard to accomplish something new without first learning something new, even if the accomplishment is limited to improving one's golf game or making furniture in the basement. But we're enthusiastic when we're working on a project we want to complete or master. The key word there is want. It has to be something we want very much to do, as opposed to those duties and projects we must do whether we like them or not.

Did you ever get a good look at a dog's face when he's chasing a rabbit? It's the happiest, most alert expression you'll ever see in your life. He's got something wonderfully worthwhile to do. And he's having the time of his life trying to do it.

You'd hardly know it was the same dog you saw snoozing and twitching on the back porch before the rabbit came into the picture; he couldn't even keep his eyes open then. It's the same with people. The rabbit may be different for each of us, but it's our job to flush it out.

Perhaps the difference is a matter of positioning. Enthusiastic people seem to be on top of life—in control of things—and have a multitude of interests. They are people who tend to be committed to something in which they find enjoyment and challenge and the satisfaction of achievement.

If you sit in a café and watch the passing crowd outside, you will see this clear-eyed oasis from time to time. There's a quickness to the step and a brightness in the eyes. If this man or woman were present in that crowd of adults Fernando Krahn depicted, he or she would be instantly recognizable. There's energy in such a person—direction, intentionality, and delight.

As for the rest—the dull-eyed, the slack-faced plodders, the survivors, we might say—they seem to be in a defensive mode vis-à-vis this business of living. They react to events; they don't cause them. They're like the fighter who has given up any hope of winning and who simply concentrates on defending himself from more injury.

The enthusiastic people are on top of life—regardless of their status; the others are on the bottom. And perhaps those on the bottom don't know about getting on top.

The word *enthusiasm* comes from the Greek word *entheos*, which means "the god within." And the happiest, most interesting people are those who have found the secret of maintaining their enthusiasm—that god within.

Our Idea of Reality

Let me quote something found in Carl Sandburg's account of the Kansas sodbuster. Who was that early sodbuster in Kansas? He leaned at the gate post and studied the horizon and figured out what corn might do next year and tried to calculate why God ever made the grasshopper, and why two days of hot winds smothered the life out of the stand of wheat, and why there was such a spread between what he got for grain and the price quoted in Chicago and New York. As he was contemplating these notions, a newcomer drove up in a covered wagon.

"What kind of folks live around here?" he asked.

"Well, stranger," said the sodbuster, "what kind of folks was there in the country you come from?"

"Well, there was mostly a low-down, lying, thieving, gossiping, backbiting lot of people."

After a few seconds of reflection, the sodbuster replied: "Well, I guess, stranger, that's about the kind of folks you'll find around here."

And the stranger had just about blended into the dusty gray cottonwoods, becoming a clump on the horizon, when another newcomer drove up.

"What kind of folks live around here?" the stranger asked.

And again the sodbuster replied, "Well, stranger, what kind of folks was there in the country you come from?"

The friendly stranger said with a smile: "Well, there was mostly a decent, hardworking, law-abiding, friendly lot of people."

And again the sodbuster said, "Well, I guess, stranger, that's about the kind of folks you'll find around here."

And the second wagon moved off and blended with the dusty gray cottonwoods on the horizon while the early sodbuster leaned at his gatepost and tried to figure out why two days of hot winds smothered the life out of a nice stand of wheat.

Noel McGinnis tells us that what Carl Sandburg means here is that the world cooperates with us by conforming to our expectations of it. The classic example of this, of course, is the paranoid person who suspects that everyone's against him and who, therefore, relates to people in such a way that they're bound to be against him.

Psychologists have demonstrated that our idea of reality is determined by our perception of things—the way our senses interpret things—rather than the way things really are. Edward T. Hall has written that the relationship between man and the cultural dimension is one in which both man and his environment participate in molding each other. Man is now in the position of actually creating the total world in which he lives. In creating this world, he is actually determining what kind of an organism he'll be.

Carl Sandburg, Dorothy Lee, Benjamin Lee Whorf, Edward Hall, and numerous others have told us in essence that we create our own space. Now, what does this mean? Well, as with Albert Einstein, it means that space is relative. Unlike Newtonian physicists, Einstein did not conceive of space as an absolute entity in relation to which things were organized. Quite the contrary, he defines space as the relationship that exists among things as a result of their organization.

Well, the tendency for reality to be a self-fulfilling prophecy rather than an absolute given has been explained by some modern anthropologists. Dorothy Lee does a good job of it in *Freedom and Culture*. And what all this means for you and me is that our individual worlds will respond to us in the way in which we see them. They will become for us what we expect of them. We are the creators of our own surroundings.

Keeping the Luster in Your Life

People who allow themselves to get in a rut usually don't realize that a rut is little more than a grave with both ends knocked out.

HAVE YOU EVER THOUGHT much about newness? You know, it's the quality people talk about when they say, "A new broom sweeps clean," or "Turn over a new leaf." Well newness, like most things, has its good side and its bad, depending on how we look at it.

A person in a new job, for instance, may feel he's at a disadvantage. He may be nervous, uncertain of just what he's supposed to do and just how to do it. Sometimes he's bewildered by all that's going on around him. Maybe he's even a little scared. Even so, the person who's new to a business has a unique advantage over some of the other, more seasoned women or men in the company. His job has a sparkle about it. There's a luster, a challenge in a new job that isn't always present once that position becomes familiar.

Do you remember your first day at work? I do. I can remember the first time I sat down in front of a microphone as though it were yesterday, instead of a good many years ago. Even though it was a radio station so small they used an old walk-in refrigerator for a studio, to me it was one of the most exciting days of my life. I was scared and nervous, and I sounded like a man with his neck caught in a car door, but I was thrilled, too.

How about your job? Does it still hold the excitement it did that first day? It should and it can, but does it? One of the most common mistakes we make is to let the luster fade from our lives. As it does, we gradually lose our enthusiasm, and if we're not careful we'll settle down into a worn, tired groove of boring habits. We become like oxen yoked to a mill, going around in circles with our eyes fixed only on the worn path of our feet.

People who allow themselves to get in a rut usually don't realize that a rut is little more than a grave with both ends knocked out. Now how can we stay out of this deadly rut? How can we keep our enthusiasm and maintain the luster in our lives instead of allowing it to fade with time and familiarity? The answer lies in reminding ourselves of things we already know but sometimes tend to forget.

A Chicago executive once told me how he maintained the luster in his job, how he charged his batteries during the early days of his career. Whenever over-familiarity with his product and service or the negativity of some of his prospects or associates began to undermine his enthusiasm for what he was selling, he'd simply make a service call on one of his best customers. There he could reassure himself of the excellent results being realized through the use of his company's products. Then my friend would head out again with renewed confidence in himself, in his ability to be of service, and in the benefits he could deliver to every new prospect.

You see, even though the everyday details of our work may seem old hat to us, we should remember that those we serve look forward eagerly to the product or service. A person may be indifferent about many things, but the things he spends his money on aren't among them.

We shouldn't be indifferent either, and we won't be if we look at our product or service through the eyes of a happy customer.

People are on stage every day. Like the actors in a Broadway play, they're sometimes required to say the same words and go through the same basic actions day after day and week after week. The professional actor learns his lines and movements and then performs the part every day, often twice a day, for as long as the play will run. He can never allow himself to become bored with the role any more than we can afford to become bored with our work. The actor knows his audience is a new one for every performance. What he is doing isn't boring to them.

What does the actor do to main enthusiasm, to keep excitement in his acting? He studies and works. He continues to improve his role. He lives his part, constantly refining his timing and movements, forever finding ways to put even greater meaning into the words he must say.

All of us are in the people business. Each day we have the opportunity to learn firsthand one of life's most valuable lessons: how to get along well with people, how to make friends with those with whom we work, and how to persuade them to make decisions that will benefit both them and ourselves. Our success in most any type of activity will always be in exact ratio to our ability to influence people.

And the best way I know to influence people is to care enough, to know enough, to serve them well. Sometimes we lose sight of the value of our work and when we do, we lose the luster—not just from our work, but from our lives. So here are some more luster-restoring ideas you can use right now and every day from now on.

1. Understand that anything, no matter how exciting in the beginning, will grow—not *may* grow, but *will* grow—stale in time if we're not careful.

2. Keep in mind that fighting off staleness in our lives is a daily job. There's something you can— something you *must* do—every day in order to keep vitality in your performance. It is simply the actor's technique: live the part.

3. Realize that there's no such thing as a job without a future. Every job has a future just as every person has. Whether or not that future is great or small depends entirely upon the person holding it.

4. See the big picture. See your work in relation to the whole scheme of things. Your work is

important to those you serve. Your success will
depend on how well you provide that service.

5. Finally, keep developing your ability to see your-
    self and your work through the eyes of that most
    important person, the recipient. And remember,
    don't ever lose the luster.

Turning Problems into Projects

WHEN WE USE A EUPHEMISM, we use a word that is perhaps less expressive or direct but often less distasteful or less
offensive than another. When we say a person has "passed away"
instead of saying he has "died," we are speaking euphemistically. In
that particular case, it's less than ideal, but euphemisms, properly
used, can change one's entire outlook on a situation.

My old friend, Parky Parkinson, reminded me that by changing
the word "problem" to "project," we can change our attitude toward
the situation.

The great Arctic explorer, Roald Amundsen, said that he and his
men could never have gotten through the situations they faced if
they had not given them euphemistic names. These euphemisms
took some of the strangeness, the hazard, the challenge—even the
terror—out of their experiences.

A problem might seem ominous or threatening, but if we call it a "project" instead, our approach to it changes; we view it as something that has a solution—a solution we are engaged in finding. In the same way, we can remind ourselves that our opportunities are often in exact proportion to our problems. Polio was a problem worldwide, but to Dr. Jonas Salk and his fellow researchers it was a project on which they were working and which they were successful in solving. Cancer is a problem to millions worldwide, but it's a project to thousands of hardworking people in the sciences, and it will be overcome.

When we have a pressing problem—and who is without one for long?—I think we need to take this intelligent attitude toward it. This is not a Pollyanna attitude, unless you want to call all the people who have been solving human problems for centuries Polyannas. It is, rather, a very human, intelligent attitude.

Following an operation one time, I had to go back to my surgeon for checkups, which involved a very painful re-examination of the work he'd done. At first, I would holler and curse and tell him it hurt like you-know-what. But he would just smile benignly and say, "No, that's stimulating!" It still hurt, but thinking of it as stimulating did something to make the situation a bit less serious and painful, and we could laugh about it.

What might seem like a forthcoming problem might be termed an "adventure" instead. Thinking of the move to a strange community and a new job as an adventure could change one's attitude toward it. And it's our attitude toward something that, more than anything else, will determine its successful outcome.

So try changing the words you use for situations normally thought of as bad or threatening or painful to euphemisms, which can give you a more positive outlook. Think of them as projects or adventures, and go tearing into them, looking for solutions. It's all a matter of semantics and attitude.

Problems are a necessary and an unending part of living. Our job is to solve them for as long as we can. And solve them we do.

TRANSFORMATIONAL LIVING

How do you react to the problems in your life?

Have you ever looked for opportunities that might stem from the problems you face?

Can you think of a way to reframe your problem so that it becomes an adventure?

Chapter Two

MASTERING YOUR SELF-IMAGE

Creating Your Greatest Image

IMAGINE THAT YOU are seated in a theater, looking at the curtain that hides the blank screen as you wait for the movie to begin.

What will this movie do for you? How will it affect you? What impact will it have on your life?

Will you feel moved—perhaps even to tears? Will you laugh at a comedy or feel terrified at the crises faced by the hero or heroine? Will you feel wonderful waves of love and compassion or surges of resentment?

All these feelings will pulse through you—and more. For the movie you will see is about the most fascinating person in the world—yourself.

In this theater, which is in the mind and heart of each of us, you are the producer, director, writer, actor or actress, hero, and the villain. You are the film technician up in the booth and the audience that reacts to this thrilling drama.

The exciting story unfolding upon this inner screen is one that is invented every second of your life—yesterday, tomorrow, but most importantly, right now.

You watch the image on that screen, and you invent the image on that screen—right now. Will the story have a happy ending? Is it full of happiness and success or sorrow and failure? The storyline is already there, and the discerning eye can tell the direction in which the story will go.

But one realization can comfort you: because you are the dramatist, the director, and the actor, you can change the story as it unfolds. Now. This instant. And for your whole lifetime.

You can make this a success story. You can be the hero and conquer the villain. And you can make this a heart-warming story that will enrich the lives of all who know you, rather than a drab, mechanical tale, a chronicle of boredom.

It's all inside you. It all depends on what you do with an image you carry inside you, an image that is your most important tool for good or for ill. It all depends on you—and your self-image.

The self-image is your own conception of the sort of person you are. It is a product of past experiences, successes and failures, humiliations and triumphs, and the way other people react to you, especially in early childhood. From these factors, and from others, you build up a picture of yourself that you believe is true. The picture may be false—and in many cases is false—but the important fact here is that you act just as if it were true. For all intents and purposes, it is true.

If it's a good, healthy, successful self-image, fine. But if it can stand some improvement, you can change it for the better and start getting the kind of results such a change will bring about.

The Positive Use of Imagination

We form a mental picture of ourselves through experience, and we can change that picture the same way—through experience.

OUR THOUGHTS, HABITS, AND EVEN OUR ABILITIES must be those of the person we believe ourselves to be. We can set new limits in place of old ones. But we can't surpass the limits of our current self-image.

There's a story about a Wisconsin farmer who was walking through his fields one day when he stumbled over a little glass jug in his pumpkin patch. Out of curiosity he poked the young pumpkin through the neck of the jug, being careful not to break the vine, then he placed his little experiment back on the ground and walked away. When harvest time came, the farmer was working his way down a row of big, ripe pumpkins when he again came upon the glass jug. But this time it looked different. Picking it up, he discovered that the young pumpkin he'd poked inside now completely filled its glass prison. Having no more room, it had stopped growing. The farmer broke the jug and held in his hand a runt pumpkin, less than half the size of all the other pumpkins and exactly the shape of the jug.

Well, people aren't pumpkins, but our self-image is something like that jug. It determines the size and kind of person we become. The similarity ends with the fact that we can remove our self-imposed limitations by enlarging our self-image. We form a mental picture of ourselves through experience, and we can change that picture the same way—through experience. If the actual experience we need is not available to us, we can, according to self-image psychology, create that experience synthetically. Now scientists agree that the human nervous system is incapable of distinguishing between actual experience and the same experience imagined vividly and in complete detail.

Worry is a good example of this synthetic experience. When a person worries about something, he projects himself mentally, emotionally, and even physically into a situation that hasn't even occurred.

The man who worries intensely about failure finds himself experiencing the same reactions that accompany actual failure: feelings of anxiety, inadequacy, and humiliation, and eventually headaches and an upset stomach. As far as his mind and body are concerned, he has failed. And if he worries about it long enough, if he concentrates on failure intensely enough, he will upset himself to the extent that he will fail and he'll get sick.

Now, everything can be used in either one of two ways: positively or negatively, constructively or destructively. Worry is the negative use of creative imagination. It's a negative synthetic experience. But most people apparently never realize that positive results, just as real as the negative results of worry, can be achieved through using our imagination constructively.

The man who worries about failure is unwittingly defeating himself. He is feeding his mind the wrong data. If he spent the same amount of time visualizing success as he spends thinking about failure, he could reverse the process of synthetic experience. Instead of anxiety, he could develop confidence, self-assurance, and poise, and a feeling of well-being would replace apprehension. By concentrating on the success he desires, by synthetically experiencing that success, he could expand his self-image into that of a person for whom success is normal and expected.

Why not practice holding the self-image of the person you most want to become? This is the person you can become. Use your spare moments to concentrate on your goals and the greater success you seek. Analyze your past successes, and formulate ways your success can be increased in the future.

Put more into the positive use of your imagination than you ever put into its negative use, worry. You're merely reversing the same creative process. Now it's working for you instead of against you.

Nobody pokes us into the glass prisons beyond which we can't grow. But all too often, almost unknowingly, we set unnecessary limits for ourselves by holding a self-image that's restricted, inadequate for the full realization of our potentialities.

Each of us is, at this moment, the product of all his or her thoughts and experiences and environment up to this point. Through thought we can control to an almost unbelievable degree both our experience and our environment from here on. Whether or not we choose to direct our own course through life is entirely up to us. The important thing is to know that it can be done.

Four Steps to a Healthy Self-Image

ONE TIME THE LATE DR. MAXWELL MALTZ, whom we called Uncle Max, dropped by my office for a chat and lunch. We got to talking on his favorite subject—namely, how a person can come to grips with himself, develop a healthy self-image, and find freedom in the world.

He told me he had discovered four important steps that a person can take on a regular basis to form the new habits that can build a healthy, new self-image. As he talked at lunch, I made notes on a scrap of paper. Here are his four points in the order in which he gave them to me:

1. **Forgive others, with no strings attached.** You must clean the slate absolutely, forgiving every person against whom you might hold some kind of grudge. You do this for your own sake, your own peace of mind. We don't hurt others when we hold hatred toward them; we hurt ourselves—seriously. It can lead to serious illness. So, number one, forgive others—all others. If you cannot take this first step, you can forget the rest; you haven't grown up yet.

2. **Forgive yourself.** See yourself with kind eyes. Try to forget completely all the idiotic things you've done, the pain you've given to others, the embarrassments you've suffered, the mistakes you've made in the past. Again, wipe clean the slate, and forgive yourself. "Look in the mirror," he said, "and forgive yourself." Practice this, and you can actually pull it off. It's not easy to forgive ourselves. We tend to be much tougher on ourselves than we are on others. But the fact is, blame doesn't help; it's a destructive emotion.

3. **See yourself at your best.** As Dr. Maltz put it, "We can start the day in frustration or confidence; take your pick." The intelligent thing to do is pick confidence, if it's at all possible. There are bad days, but it's better to begin the day in a confident mood than in a mood of frustration.

4. **Keep up with yourself.** Don't worry about what others are doing or what others have done or have.

Keep your own pace; it's different from the pace of others. It's faster than some, slower than others. Forget the Joneses, and don't feel guilty about moving ahead of some of your contemporaries. The person who deliberately holds himself down to a slower pace just to be one of the gang is a fool. Keep up with yourself. Live the life you want to live. Earn what you want to earn. Do what you want to do. Live your own life, and don't be too concerned about how others are living theirs.

Four steps to a healthy self-image: (1) forgive others; (2) forgive yourself; (3) see yourself at your best—choose confidence instead of frustration; and (4) keep up with yourself—march to your own drummer, and don't worry about what others are doing.

TRANSFORMATIONAL LIVING

Are you holding a grudge against someone in your life?

Are you able to look in the mirror and feel good about what you see?

Are you focused squarely on your own achievements instead of how much you achieve in relation to others?

How to Restore Your Self-Esteem

IN HIS BOOK, *Psycho-Cybernetics*, Dr. Maxwell Maltz wrote:

"Of all the traps and pitfalls in life, self-disesteem is the deadliest and the hardest to overcome; for it is a pit designed and dug by our own hands, summed up in the phrase, 'It's no use—I can't do it.'

"The penalty of succumbing to it is heavy—both for the individual in terms of material rewards lost and for society in gains and progress unachieved.

[...]

"On those days when we are most subject to...'fearful unbelief' [in ourselves], when we most doubt ourselves and feel inadequate to our task—isn't it precisely then that we are most difficult to get along with?

"We simply must get it through our heads that holding a low opinion of ourselves is not a virtue but a vice. Jealousy, for example, which is the scourge of many a marriage, is nearly always caused by self-doubt. The person with adequate self-esteem doesn't feel hostile toward others. He isn't out to prove anything. He can see facts more clearly, isn't as demanding in his claims on other people.

"The housewife who felt that a facelift might cause her husband and children to appreciate her more really needed to appreciate herself more. Middle age, plus a few wrinkles and a few gray hairs, had caused her to lose her self-esteem. She then became supersensitive to innocent remarks and actions of her family."

And here's Dr. Maxwell Maltz's prescription for restoring your self-esteem: "Stop carrying around a mental picture of yourself as a defeated, worthless person. Stop dramatizing yourself as an object of pity and injustice.

[...]

"The word *esteem* literally means 'to appreciate the worth of.' Why do men stand in awe of the stars and the moon, the immensity of the sea, the beauty of a flower or a sunset, and at the same time downgrade themselves? Did not the same Creator make man? Is not man himself the most marvelous creation of all? This appreciation of your own worth is not egotism unless you assume that you made yourself and should take the credit. Do not downgrade the product merely because you haven't used it correctly. Don't childishly blame the product for your own errors like the schoolboy who said, 'This typewriter can't spell.'

"But the biggest secret of self-esteem is this: Begin to appreciate other people more; show respect for any human being merely because he is a child of God and therefore a thing of value. You're dealing with a unique, individual creation of the Creator of all. Practice treating other people as if they had some value—and surprisingly enough your own self-esteem will go up. For real self-esteem is not derived from the great things you've done, the things you own, or the mark you've made, but an appreciation of yourself for what you are."

If you're lacking in self-esteem, it's because you don't understand who or what you really are. If you'll take the time to learn more about yourself, you'll be delighted at what you discover.

Be an Actor, Not a Reactor

Nobody is unhappier than the perpetual reactor. His center of emotional gravity is not rooted within himself, where it belongs, but in the world outside him.

SYDNEY HARRIS BEGAN HIS "Strictly Personal" column back in 1943. He had a number of books published—all of which I think I own and enjoy. One of my favorite columns was one in which he told about walking with a friend of his to the newsstand. His friend bought a paper, thanking the vendor politely. The vendor didn't even acknowledge it.

"A sullen fellow, isn't he?" Harris commented.

"Oh, he's that way every night," shrugged his friend.

"Then why do you continue being so polite to him?" Sydney Harris asked.

"Why not?" inquired his friend. "Why should I let him decide how I'm going to act?"

As Harris thought about the incident later, it occurred to him that the operating work was *act*. His friend *acts* toward people. Many of us *react* toward them.

He has a sense of inner balance lacking in many of us frail and uncertain creatures; he knows who he is, what he stands for, and how he should behave. No boor is going to disturb the equilibrium of his nature; he simply refuses to return incivility with incivility, because then he would no longer be in command of his own conduct but a mere responder to others.

When we are enjoined in the Bible to return good for evil, we look upon this as a moral injunction, which it is; but it is also a psychological prescription for our emotional health.

Nobody is unhappier than the perpetual reactor. His center of emotional gravity is not rooted within himself, where it belongs, but in the world outside him. His spiritual temperature is always being raised or lowered by the social climate around him, and he is a mere creature at the mercy of these elements. Praise gives him a feeling of euphoria, which is false because it does not last and it does not come from self-approval. Criticism depresses him more than it should, because it confirms his own secretly shaky opinion of himself. Snubs hurt him, and the merest suspicion of unpopularity in any quarter rouses him to bitterness or aggressiveness or querulousness.

Only a saint, of course, never reacts. But a serenity of spirit cannot be achieved until we become the masters of our own actions and attitudes and not merely reactors of other people's feelings. To let another determine whether we shall be rude or gracious, elated or depressed, is to relinquish control over our own personalities, which is ultimately all we possess. The only true possession is self-possession.

Chapter Three

MANAGING YOUR INNER WORLD

The Advantages of Calmness

HERE'S SOMETHING THAT WE SHOULD READ or listen to once a day for the next forty-five years. It was written back at the turn of the century by William George Jordan. He was editor of several magazines during his lifetime, including the *Ladies Home Journal* and *The Saturday Evening Post*. He wrote, "Calmness is the rarest quality in human life. It is the poise of a great nature, in harmony with itself and its ideals. It is the moral atmosphere of a life self-reliant and self-controlled. Calmness is singleness of purpose, absolute confidence, and conscious power ready to be focused in an instant to meet any crisis.

"The Sphinx is not a true type of calmness. Petrification is not calmness; it's death—the silencing of all the energies. While no one lives his life more fully, more intentionally, and more consciously than the person who's calm, the fatalist is not calm. He's the coward's slave of his environment, hopelessly surrendering to his present condition, recklessly indifferent to his future. He accepts his life as a rudderless ship drifting on the ocean of time. He has no compass, no chart, no known port to which he is sailing. His self-confessed inferiority to all nature is shown in his existence of constant surrender. It is not calmness.

"The person who is calm has his course in life clearly marked on his chart. His hand is ever on the helm. Storm, fog, night, tempest, danger, hidden reefs—he's prepared and ready for them. He's made calm and serene by the realization that in these crises of his voyage, he needs a clear mind and a cool head, then he has nothing to do but do each day the best he can by the light he has; that he will never flinch or falter for a moment; that though he may have to tack and leave his course for a time, he'll keep ever headed toward his harbor. When he will reach it, how he will reach it, matters not to him. He rests in calmness knowing he done his best.

"When the worries and cares of the day fret you and begin to wear upon you and you chafe under the friction, be calm. Stop. Rest for a moment, and let calmness and peace assert themselves. If you let these irritating outside influences get the better of you, you're confessing your inferiority to them by permitting them to dominate you. When the tongue of malice and slander, the persecution of inferiority, tempt you to retaliate; when for an instant you forget yourself so far as to hunger for revenge, be calm. When the grey heron is pursued by its enemy, the eagle, it does not run to escape. It remains calm, takes a dignified stand, and waits quietly, facing the enemy unmoved. With a terrific force with which the eagle makes its attack, the boasted king of birds is often impaled and run through on the quiet, lance-like bill of the heron. No person in the world ever attempted to wrong another without being injured in return some way, somehow, some time. Remain calm."

Now all of that was written at the turn of the century and in language that today might sound a bit affected and archaic. It's a good message. If ever there were a quality needed in the crisis-filled world of today, it's calmness—and the kind of clear thinking calmness produces.

I wonder how improved our days would be if we would make it a point to go over that little message every morning.

***

What to Do When You Feel Inferior

THE WORDS "KNOW THYSELF" are still two of the most important words ever put together. Do you know why people sometimes—quite often, as a matter of fact—have inferiority complexes? It's because their thinking is based on a false premise. The false premise is that they compare themselves to other people, when this is actually something they should never do, since no two human beings are alike. Everybody on earth is inferior to everyone else on earth in certain areas and superior in other areas.

A wise man once wrote, "To be human is to feel inferior." This is why the well-adjusted person, the person who knows himself, isn't bothered because he can't dance as well as so-and-so, or play golf or bridge as well as someone else. It would be completely impossible for any one human being to be as good at everything as every other human being.

The well-adjusted person admires others for their talents and abilities without feeling envious. In fact, he doesn't bring himself into comparison at all. He is happily resigned to the fact that he is not the best-looking, best-built, smartest, most talented, fastest, cleverest, funniest, most engaging person on earth.

Without even thinking about it, he seems to know that every person is a potpourri of strengths and weaknesses inherited from all his ancestors. No two of them were alike, but each one had a slightly different strong point with the standard collection of weaknesses.

In his fine book *Psycho-Cybernetics*, Dr. Maxwell Maltz wrote, "Inferiority and superiority are reverse sides of the same coin. The cure lies in realizing that the coin itself is spurious...you are not 'inferior' [or] are not 'superior.' You are simply you.

"You as a personality are not in competition with any other personality simply because there is not another person on the face of the earth like you or in your particular class. You are an individual. You are unique. You are not 'like' any other person. You are not 'supposed' to be like any other person, and no other person is 'supposed' to be like you."

The doctor went on to write, "God did not create a standard person and in some way label that person by saying, 'This is it.' He made every human being individual and unique, just as He made every snowflake individual and unique.

"God created short people and fat people, black, yellow, red, and white people. He has never indicated any preference for any one size, shape or color. Abraham Lincoln once said, 'God must have loved the common people, for He made so many of them.' He was wrong. There is no 'common man'—no standardized, common pattern. He would have been nearer the truth had he said, 'God must have loved uncommon people, for He made so many of them.'"

Anybody could make himself feel inferior if he didn't realize that he is unlike any other human being who ever lived on earth. If he understands—fully and completely, intellectually and emotionally—that he is a unique and different individual, he cannot have an inferiority complex. How could he, since there's no standard against which to judge if every person is different? And every person is different.

Nothing on earth happens purely by accident. A person is living because he was meant to live, and he has talents and abilities that are his own—unique with him. His job, then, as a person is to learn to know himself. If he does, he will like himself, for he will discover he's quite a person after all. He will recognize and accept the things he cannot do as well as some other people, but he will also understand and appreciate those things it has been given him to do well. He will accept himself for what he really is—one of a kind, as different from every other person on earth as his fingerprints or his signature.

A human being is the finest, the noblest, the most godlike creature ever produced on earth. Not to be thankful for such a gift is the worst kind of ignorance. And an inferiority complex is a phantom—a ghost with no real substance. In the light of knowledge, it disappears.

The Wonders of Praise

We should try to find some way to commend those we love every day. Praise to a human being represents what sunlight, water, and soil are to a plant—the climate in which he grows best.

ONE DAY A FEW YEARS BACK, I stopped my car for gas at a service station in Hollywood, California. While the middle-aged owner of the station cheerfully went about taking care of my car's needs, I noticed the station, although not new, was spotlessly clean. I was particularly surprised at the driveway—it was as clean as if my car was the first to use it.

I asked the owner how in the world he managed to keep the driveway spotless with dozens of cars dropping oil and tracking the dirt of the highways on it. He told me how a common product, sold in every supermarket, was in his estimation the best driveway cleaner in the world. He beamed in response to my comment on the way he kept his place of business. It was a valuable moment for both of us: I learned something of value, and he experienced the pleasure of honest praise.

The need for praise is basic to everyone. With it, a person blooms and grows. Without it, he tends to shrink and withdraw into himself.

We all know children need constant praise and encouragement. When a child brings home a piece of artwork that looks for all the world like an unfortunate accident, he still expects an encouraging word. But his need for encouragement is no less than his mother's or father's. Far too many parents are not getting any praise, or at least not nearly enough.

Understanding the importance of self-esteem and seeing the never-ending need for reaffirmation of a person's worth, we should make it our business to watch for honest opportunities to give praise—especially to the members of our families and those with whom we work.

There is a subtle but enormously valuable byproduct or backfire to this sort of thing: In order to praise others, we need to look for the good. It forces us to concentrate on what's right with people and the things they do rather than on what's wrong. It focuses our attention on the positive side of the ledger and, as a result, makes us happier, more productive, and more pleasant to be around. Then, too, people like those who praise them and recognize their value. When we give praise, we attract a larger circle of friends. And finally, giving praise is the best known way to receive it. It's hard for anyone to compliment a chronic grouch.

Whenever you hear someone say, "Nobody appreciates me; nobody gives me credit for all I do," the chances are he is so wrapped up in himself and in getting happiness from others, he has completely forgotten how to give.

We should try to find some way to commend those we love every day. Praise to a human being represents what sunlight, water, and soil are to a plant—the climate in which he grows best. He does not just want it; he needs it as he needs the air he breathes.

Molière said, "The most agreeable recompense which we can receive for things which we have done is to see them known, to have them applauded with praises which honor us."

Why You Don't Have to Be a Loner

MY FATHER WAS A REGULAR and an avid reader of the old Zane Grey books (that's how I got hold of them), which invariably, or so it seemed, began with a stranger riding into town. He was tall, lean, and always covered with alkali dust. Cool gray eyes peered evenly from under straight brows, and his hand hovered near the six-gun strapped to his thigh.

He had no friends or acquaintances and seemed to like it that way. He was a man of few words and kept his own counsel. His world consisted of little more than himself and his horse and the bad guy he was usually after.

It makes a good story, and everyone seems to be intrigued by this sort of man of mystery. But, in real life, it's a lonely way to live, especially since few of us have horses these days.

You cannot know too many people. And we'd all be better off if we could overcome our natural timidity where strangers are concerned, if we could open up more.

As a friend of mine who has attained an unusually high position in the world says, "Open the doors and windows of your mind and heart to others, and you'll reap a wonderful harvest of friends."

Many of us have a tendency to speak or smile only after another person has spoken or smiled at us first. We tend to be reactive instead of proactive. It reminds me of the person who sat in front of the cold stove and said, "Give me heat, and then I'll add the wood."

The world just doesn't work that way. With a little effort, a person can form the habit of smiling and saying "hello" first. Nineteen times out of twenty, you'll get a favorable response.

I know a man who was the foreign representative for an American electronics firm. He was something of an introvert, and on his frequent flights all over the world, he'd bury himself in a book to keep from having to talk to the passenger next to him.

On one trip, a friendly Englishman managed to get a conversation started with him. It turned out that the Englishman was on an electronics buying trip to the States, and a large order resulted. Then and there he decided to change his attitude toward strangers. While it may not result in another business deal, he's meeting all sorts of interesting people and making many new friends.

We should never say, "He's not my kind of person" or "That's not my sort of crowd." Wherever there's a human being, there's a human story, and it's invariably interesting and informative. It stretches our minds, broadens our horizons, and adds to our collection of acquaintances and friends.

And all it takes is a smile, the word "hello," and a comment or two to get a conversation going. The chances are that the other person is as anxious to add to his collection of friends as we are. But he or she may be just a little on the timid side, as many people are in the presence of strangers. It's true: you can't know too many people. As we grow older, we should cultivate all the friends we can.

The person who shuts others out of his life ends up shutting himself in. Try my friend's advice. Throw open the doors and windows of your mind and heart to others, and reap a harvest of friends.

Who wants to live with a horse?

The Strength to Be Happy

It is in the expectation of happiness that much of happiness itself is found. And it takes courage to expect happiness.

O N THE OCCASION of his seventy-fifth birthday, Mark Van Doren, the American writer, poet, critic, and educator, was interviewed by a reporter for *LIFE Magazine*, and one of the things he said stuck in my mind. I saved this.

He said, "It takes courage to be happy." Now in those six words he said a great deal. Any person can wallow in misery and self-pity. It's easy to rail against the world and its injustices. It's easier still to sit down and do nothing like the famous hound dog with its tail in the crack, but it takes courage to be happy.

When he said it takes courage to be happy, he didn't mean happiness today or tomorrow or a week from next Thursday. He meant to be happy as a general, relatively constant way of living; to be a happy person as opposed to a generally unhappy person. And it does take courage—courage of a high order. The world is full, it seems, of the "it's too good to last" or "it's just my kind of luck" people who expect bad luck and rejection as confidently as they expect the sun to rise the next morning. They are people who were given bleak and disappointing starts in life.

Tolstoy said, "Man is meant for happiness and this happiness is in him, in the satisfaction of the daily needs of his existence." And La Rochefoucauld said, "Happiness is in the taste and not in the things themselves. We're happy from possessing what we like, not from possessing what others like."

In a passage that I think is very revealing, Jane Austin wrote, "No temper could be more cheerful than hers or possess in a greater degree that sanguine expectation of happiness, which is happiness itself." It is in the expectation of happiness that much of happiness itself is found. And it takes courage to expect happiness.

Balzac wrote, "All happiness depends on courage and work." I've had many periods of wretchedness, but with energy and, above all, with illusions, I've pulled through them all.

My old favorite, George Santayana said, "Happiness is the only sanction in life. Where happiness fails, existence remains a mad and lamentable experiment."

Bertrand Russell put it well when he said, "Contempt for happiness is usually contempt for other people's happiness and is an elegant disguise for hatred of the human race."

The Chinese philosopher, Lin Yutang, said, "I've always been impressed by the fact that the most studiously avoided subject in Western philosophy is that of happiness."

A French philosopher said much the same as did Mark Van Doren. He said, "To live, we must conquer incessantly. We must have the courage to be happy."

We've all seen people seriously handicapped in one way or another who are wonderfully cheerful and happy people. And we've wondered how they do it. We've said to ourselves, "I don't think I could be happy if I had his or her affliction." These people are happy because they are courageous and because they don't like the alternative.

Chapter Four

LIBERATE THE POWER
OF YOUR MIND

The Truth of the Mind

IN JOHN MILTON'S *Paradise Lost*, Satan says, "The mind is its own place and in itself can make a heaven of hell, a hell of heaven." When Satan says this, he does not realize its truth or the ironic fact that his hate-filled mind has indeed made for him "a hell of heaven" but cannot make a "heaven of hell." And Satan, in this great work by Milton, has lots of company. Read that line again: "The mind in its own place and in itself can make a heaven of hell, a hell of heaven."

No one knows or can even guess at the uncounted millions who are living in a virtual heaven of opportunity in every department of their lives and yet turn it into a living hell. They have every opportunity to love, and yet they hate. They have every opportunity to trust, and yet they mistrust.

They have every opportunity to work and give of themselves. Yet they hold back in the suspicious dread that they're being cheated. They have every opportunity to share in the wealth of the richest society since the beginning of the world, yet they sit and grumble because it's not given to them for being lazy and ignorant. They're ignorant even though they are surrounded on every side, with a free and abundant opportunity to learn their full capacity. The public libraries in their towns and cities are half empty waiting in vain for them to enter and learn. The schools and their parents begged them to stay in schools, to qualify themselves for a fast-changing world, but they drop out.

But it's not just the sum of these that the mind turns a possible heaven into a hell. In every walk of life, in every strata of society, you can see the bitter, desolate expressions; the hollow eyes; and the listless hands of those whose minds have condemned them to the tortures of the damned or a life of endless tedium and ennui.

The Roman Seneca put it this way: "A great, a good, and a right mind is a kind of divinity lodged in flesh and may be the blessing of a slave as well as of a prince. It came from heaven and to heaven it must return. And it's a kind of heavenly felicity which a pure and virtuous mind enjoys, in some degree even on earth."

As Chaucer said, "My mind to me a kingdom is. Such present joys therein I find that it excels all other bliss that earth affords. Every person's mind is his kingdom. And he as the reigning monarch decides what kind of a kingdom it is to be: bleak or bountiful, rich or poor, interesting or dull, happy or unhappy."

And the most important moment of our lives is when we understand that we can fashion our minds as we will.

George Berkeley said, "What stubbing, plowing, digging, and harrowing is to land, that thinking, reflecting, examining is to the mind." We know the soil is rich. The harvest is up to us.

The Remedy for an Anxious Mind

FEW PEOPLE IN THE HISTORY of the world had more responsibility in their hands, or greater crises to face, than Winston Churchill during the years when he was prime minister of England. He was able to stand up to the kinds of problems that would have killed a dozen lesser men because of a system he developed early in his life—a system for relieving worry and tension. It can be invaluable for us today.

He wrote, "Many remedies are suggested for the avoidance of worry and mental overstrain by persons who, over prolonged periods, have to bear exceptional responsibilities and discharge duties upon a very large scale. Some advise exercise, and others, retreat. Some praise solitude, and others, gaiety. No doubt all these may play their part according to the individual temperament. But the element which is constant and common in all of them is change.

"Change is the master key. A man can wear out a particular part of his mind by continually using it and tiring of it, just in the same way he can wear out the elbows of his coat. There is, however, this difference between the living cells of the brain and inanimate articles: One cannot mend the frayed elbows of a coat by rubbing the sleeves or shoulders, but the tired parts of the mind can be rested and strengthened not merely by rest but by using other parts. It is not enough merely to switch off the lights which play upon the main and ordinary field of interest; a new field of interest must be illuminated.

"It is no use saying to the tired 'mental muscles'—if one may coin such an expression, 'I will give you a good rest', 'I will go for a long walk', or, 'I will lie down and think of nothing.' The mind keeps busy just the same. If it has been weighing and measuring, it goes on weighing and measuring. If it has been worrying, it goes on worrying. It is only when new cells are called into activity, when new stars become the lords of the ascendant, that relief, repose, refreshment are afforded."

That's good advice, isn't it? Trying to shut down the mind by turning a mental switch is virtually impossible. But turning it to something new will let the tired part refresh itself. This is why golf, tennis, fishing, and other participation sports are important to good health. You can be a spectator at a sporting event and still worry, but you can't play and worry.

The trick—and this is the hard part—is to force yourself to do something else when your mind is full of worry or is tired from one kind of work. This knack must be developed, and Winston Churchill developed it. During the darkest days of World War II, when the Allies were losing on every front, Churchill could rest his mind by turning it to some entirely new activity and giving it his complete attention. He did this just as you or I would take the medicine prescribed by a doctor; he did it to keep well. He could then return to the problems of the world with his mind rested and refreshed.

Doctors have said many times that it isn't overwork that kills people; it's over-worry until the mind becomes discouraged and just gives out.

Dr. Charles Mayo said, "Worry affects the circulation—the heart, the glands, the whole nervous system. I have never known anyone who died from overwork but many who died from doubt."

Learning about Thinking

There is a force—call it what you will—that seems to come to the aid of those who develop a healthy attitude about thinking and getting ideas and moving toward difficult goals. Sometimes we call it "getting lucky," but that's not what it really is.

THERE WAS AN ENGLISH SCHOOLMASTER who made it a point to ask every child coming to his school, "Do you know why you need to go to school?"

The children would usually just stare back at him, as overwhelmed by him as by the question. And he would answer, "You go to school so you will learn to think."

My old friend Louis Atkinson of Tooele, Utah, called me recently and told me he had talked to his three-year-old son, Craig, about that and about the importance of learning to think. The subject of thinking and what it can mean is brought up often between the two of them when they're together, working in the garden or in the evening. And Louis said, "One night we went into Craig's room to get him ready for bed, and little Craig commented, 'Thinking helps make you happy. And that's very important!'"

There was quick agreement there, and the young philosopher went to bed.

Louis Atkinson is a high school teacher, and he used the story with his students.

Yes, thinking helps make you happy, and that's very important. And the more we learn, the greater our experiences, the more possibilities we put into the thinking raw material pile. And thinking is the father of creation. Thinking, to the person making plans, is the navigator of his future life. And yes, that's very important. But there's more there, too.

Louis asked me over the phone if I'd seen the motion picture *Star Wars*. I said that I had not, but I told him that I had seen, at my son's urging, the two sequels. "Do you remember the bit in there about 'the Force'?" he asked.

I said that I did remember, but more than that, I had been affected by the term as much as he had.

There is a force—call it what you will—that seems to come to the aid of those who develop a healthy attitude about thinking and getting ideas and moving toward difficult goals. Sometimes we call it "getting lucky," but that's not really what it is. It's a momentum—a force—that, like a good wave, will give you all sorts of help once you're really on your way.

It takes a long time to develop sometimes, but when it comes, we seem to be able to feel it. It gives us confidence and at the same time a sense of appreciation, a sense of gratitude. It is never accompanied by cockiness. In fact, I doubt if it can come to the shallow person.

I'm sure little Craig will learn about that, too, as he gets a bit older. But he's already big where it counts: he's learning about thinking.

Thinking It Through

MANY YEARS AGO, there were some very good small books published, written by an Irishman named William T. Reilly, PhD. One of them was titled *The Twelve Rules for Straight Thinking*, published back in 1947.

He reminds us that we cannot stop our minds from jumping to conclusions. Minds tend to do that. And often in our desire to capture the spotlight in our business or social conversations—to make a good impression on the boss maybe and prove we're in possession of quick and alert minds—we tend to jump to hasty conclusions which, in more sober consideration, turn out to be the dumbest ideas heard in that boardroom, or conference room, or social gathering in fifty years.

The trouble is that most of us easily mistake a quick solution as the best or only solution, whereas a quick answer is all too often a poor one and may often be the wrong one, which doesn't solve the problem at all. It might create new problems.

Now while we cannot keep our minds from jumping to conclusions, we can protect ourselves from the damaging effects of conclusion-jumping by using a delayed response to any serious question. That is, give ourselves time to think it through, as we should.

The delayed response is actually the first sign of intelligence—the first sign of thought. In fact, any time a person comes to you with a problem you feel you should help with, say, "Let me think about that. I don't like to make quick decisions on important matters." You're bound to make a more favorable impression.

Younger men and women in a company often feel that they have to come up with instantaneous and miraculous solutions to problems posed by their superiors. Nothing could be further from the truth. An executive has a great deal of respect for the person who says, "I want to think about this a while before I give you my best opinion."

Now you have the time to think, to back up and go through the four simple steps in straight thinking. Step one: Separate facts from opinions and analyze the facts. Step two: Define the real problem and consider possible solutions. Step three: Secure evidence on possible solutions. And step four: Weigh the evidence and arrive at a sound conclusion. You're still going to make wrong decisions even with the best system, but you'll make fewer. Ad-libbing your way through life is risky, and I think Doc Reilly has some excellent suggestions there.

When you consider a problem, think vertically for a while, that is, conventionally. If you can't come up with answers that haven't already been tried and found wanting that way, think horizontally, in totally new directions. That is, instead of just drilling the one hole deeper, look for new ground to drill. You might just find the wonderful solution out in left field. Then your superior will take credit for the idea. No, I'm just kidding. It's really the best way to go about it.

Life presents us with one problem after another all the days of our lives. Most of them don't require a great deal of thought. When they do, the delayed response is a very good idea.

How to Find New Ideas

IF A BUSINESS FIRM COULD FIND better ways to mine the brains of the people working for it, it could undoubtedly move ahead much faster and do a much better job of cutting costs and improving profits.

I read something in the *Wall Street Journal* some time back about an electronics firm that stops everything at two o'clock in the afternoon for a think session attended by its top design engineers. The doors are closed, the telephones are shut off in the conference room used for the purpose, they exchange ideas—spark each other with their thoughts of the day. Knowing the think session is coming up every day, each of the participants tries to come up with an idea or two between sessions.

A shoe company has a private "reflection period" for each company official, plus brainstorming sessions every two weeks. An official said, "It's amazing what comes out of those sessions." And another company takes a dozen top executives out of town every few months to discuss major problems.

Company officials on a business trip are often amazed at the wonderful ideas they get as soon as they leave the routine of their offices and get off together. Companies that worry about their people getting to the office on time and putting in a full day's work might be surprised and delighted at the profit-producing ideas these same people might get if they were sent off on a trip to another town for a few days and asked to get some good ideas.

Rosabeth Moss Kanter tells the story of Clarence Birdseye, the inventor of frozen vegetables. Birdseye had a produce business in New York at the turn of the century. At that time, she says, the conventional wisdom about the best way to manage a business was not so different from the conventional wisdom of today: it was "mind the store"; be there all the time. But Birdseye didn't do that. He was an adventurer, an explorer, as well as an entrepreneur, and on one of his adventure trips, he made an expedition to Labrador. It was there that he noticed that when the Eskimos froze caribou meat in the dry

Arctic air, it was still flavorful and tender when thawed and cooked months later. He adapted that idea to his produce business, and, of course, he built a great company.

Kanter says that if we're to be innovative, "we need to make periodic expeditions to Labrador. Get away. Go somewhere different. Get your thinking shaken up. See something that's different from everyday reality, something that might suggest a creative twist on the very problem you're trying to solve." She says, "Most organizations have budgets to send people to professional meetings. I've started to recommend that those companies use those budgets to send people to professional meetings in some other field—not their own—so they'll encounter new and different perspectives."

Ideas have a way of coming when we're away from the routine of our jobs. But it takes an awareness of the value of ideas and the fun of getting good ones. The experts in this field say that most people, even executives, seldom think very much between crises. That is, they use their minds defensively; they use them only when they're attacked with a problem. They seldom indulge in creative thinking between crises. This is a pity. A few minutes a day devoted to deliberate thinking can work wonders for the mind, the person and the business, and the home and family life as well.

You might give it some thought. There are gold mines between all those ears. It costs a lot of money to educate and train a person these days. It's a shame to employ only a person's physical presence and let all those wonderful brains go to pasture.

TRANSFORMATIONAL LIVING

Set aside a specific time of day for yourself when you do nothing but collect your thoughts.

Have paper and pencil handy so that you can record your ideas as you discover them.

Every so often, try to remove yourself from your familiar surroundings and everyday routines to gain a new perspective on your life.

The Genius of Daydreaming

A TEACHER, BUSY WITH INSTRUCTIONS for the next subject, noticed that one child was gazing out the window. She stopped talking, and the entire class turned to look at the daydreamer. Finally, the child realized everything was too quiet, except for an occasional snicker from another student, and turned to face the teacher.

"What have you been doing?" asked the teacher.

"I was thinking," the child replied.

The teacher snapped back, "Don't you know you're not supposed to think in school?!" whereupon, after a moment of stunned silence, the children burst into helpless laughter, much to the teacher's embarrassment.

I saw the most interesting little cartoon the other day. It depicted a class of prehistoric children, all dressed in small bearskins, sitting on the floor of a cave. Before them was the teacher, wearing a large bearskin. He had sketched a picture of a deer on the wall of the cave and had drawn a small "x" where the heart would be. He was apparently teaching a class on how to hunt a deer.

One of the small children, however, wasn't paying attention. He was sitting like the others, but he was turned toward the viewer and was whittling with a small stone knife. The teacher was giving him a bad time about not paying attention and said, "Don't you want to keep up with the other children?" And then you see that the child is whittling an airplane.

When children are thinking, they are performing the highest function of the human creature, and it can happen that they're thinking on a much higher and better plane than they would be if they were paying attention to what is presently going on.

Daydreaming is not necessarily, as popular opinion would have it, a waste of time—far from it. Daydreams have led to many of the benefits we enjoy today: books, motion pictures, conveniences of modern society, scientific breakthroughs. No one knows very much about the human brain, but when it's allowed to fly out the window and come up with what it will, it can occasionally come up with some real winners.

Of course, too much daydreaming without engineering the good ideas down to earth and putting them into use, can lead to trouble. It might be said that there is a time to daydream and a time to get to work. Certainly, if all the children in a classroom were allowed to daydream at will, nobody would ever learn anything. But we should be careful when we jump on children for thinking instead of paying attention; of the two, thinking is usually the more important, and there's altogether too little of it these days.

It seems that we tend to daydream about subjects that are important to us, and by so doing, we lay the groundwork for future activity and accomplishment. Daydreaming can also prevent illness from too much negative stress. Every serviceman who has ever gone into combat knows how daydreaming in quiet moments can take one back to one's home and family and friends. For a few moments, the war is blotted out, the anxiety and fear of injury or instant extinction are forgotten, and the world is back in order. There's no doubt that daydreaming has an important therapeutic effect.

Daydreaming is one of our greatest gifts, and we'd be much poorer without it. And when you peek into your youngster's room and find him quietly gazing out the window or at the ceiling, it might be a good idea just to leave him alone for a while.

Keeping Ideas within Reach

Once you know what you want to do, what you want to
accomplish, you will, if your desire's strong enough,
find a way to accomplish it.

AN INTERESTING AND IMPORTANT BIT of information we should keep in mind is that the idea we're looking for is never beyond our reach. I have a little sign near my typewriter that reads, "I've had my solutions for a long time. But I do not yet know how I'm to arrive at them."

It was written by the great nineteenth-century German inventor Carl Gauss. "I have had my solutions for a long time. But I do not yet know how I am to arrive at them." It means we know the point at which we intend to arrive. We just don't yet know how to get there.

Thomas Edison knew what he was looking for when he decided to invent an electric light. Once that decision was reached he was able, long and difficult as the solution was, to find the ideas he needed. You might say, "Well, not everyone would be able to do what Thomas Edison did." You'd be right, because not everyone was looking for a way to develop an electric light. In fact, people were quite content with the lights they had, just as they were perfectly happy with the horse and buggy and ridiculed early attempts to produce a workable motorcar. The point that's important to remember here is that once you know what you want to do, what you want to accomplish, you will, if your desire's strong enough, find a way to accomplish it. And the process is not all that difficult to understand.

When you make up your mind to achieve some end, whatever it happens to be, you're excited about the idea. It fills your mind and it's strengthened by your emotional involvement. How to achieve it becomes something of an obsession, and you find yourself thinking about it all the time. As you do, you're planting it, charged with the power of your emotion, deep in your subconscious, where a great and largely mysterious mental computer goes to work on it. It works on a problem below the conscious level and looks for the solution, much, I suppose, like a great electronic scanner, looking at thousands of possibilities, exploring memory, looking at new permutations. From time to time, it sends up a tentative solution. When it does, you shouldn't be too quick to accept it. You should make a note of it always and stick it in the idea file, but keep pushing the problem back down into the big tumbler. From time to time, new solutions or partial solutions will appear. Perhaps you'll try some of them and some won't work.

Finally, if you keep sending the problem back down, the glorious non-collapsible big idea you're looking for will finally be extruded, and that's it—the light works; it's the answer. From then on, it's a matter of refinement and variation.

I think the important thing to remember here is that you can get the idea you're looking for if you follow this method and stick with it. And it doesn't necessarily mean that the idea will come to you. It can come to someone else, and through him or her to you. That's what happened to Charles Darwin and many other investigators. As long as you find the solution to the problem, you don't care where it comes from. You can get just the idea for which you've been looking for months, even years, from a casual acquaintance at a business luncheon or from something you see in a magazine or a store window or read in a good book. But the idea you're looking for is never beyond your reach. Hunting for ideas you need to reach the goal you've set for yourself can be an interesting and exciting journey—a journey into meaning and discovery. And it can make living a lot of fun.

The Key to Motivation

PEOPLE ARE FOREVER ASKING, "How do you motivate a person?" People in management, teachers, and parents ask, "How does one go about bringing out more of the best in people—for their own good as well as the good of society?"

The answer to that question was given in the seventeenth century by the French scientist and philosopher, René Descartes. I forget in which of his works he said it, but I remember that he said, "Imagination is the key to motivation." And truer words were never put together.

If you would motivate a person, teach him the importance of imagination. You have only to think back to the times in your own life when you've been filled with excitement and interest and enthusiasm. Hasn't it almost always been at times when you've come up with a great idea, when your imagination is all fired up?

Imagination is a sign of youthfulness in any person, young or old. In fact, keeping the imagination active will help a person remain young in everything but years all his life.

All right, how to stimulate the imagination of others: With some people it isn't necessary; they're just naturally imaginative people who were raised in families in which imagination played a major role. But I think it's safe to say that these people—adults, I'm talking about—are rather rare. Every business has people, wonderfully talented, who can take an idea and work wonders with it. But they don't come up with ideas themselves, and let's face it, most people don't.

The way to stimulate imagination is to establish the climate for it. It is, simply, to ask for it.

One way is to point out to people that their jobs will change remarkably for the better in the years ahead as new and better ideas come along, and ask them if they can come up with some of those ideas now. Why wait for someone else to come up with the good ideas; maybe we can come up with them first.

Another way is to make sure people are made a part of new plans; that they feel their ideas and contributions are needed and important, that they're vital members of the team.

A few years ago, a large oil company asked its salespeople to give some thought and come up with some answers to this question: What will the service station be like ten years from now? Management was amazed and delighted by the answers. These people calling on service stations every day were eminently qualified to give some intelligent and exciting answers to that question.

The same sort of thing will work with any group, and it will add new interest to the job. Suggestion systems are fine and have made great contributions, but they're largely passive. The best way to stimulate ideas and imagination is to ask questions, to ask for help.

As for management people themselves, studies seem to indicate that they seldom bother to think very much between crises. They, too, need stimulation in the imagination department.

René Descartes was right. The key to motivation is imagination, whether we're motivating others or ourselves. When imagination is working, boredom and stagnation disappear.

Capturing Your Ideas

IDEAS, AND ESPECIALLY THE REALLY GOOD ONES, are fragile, evanescent things. They flit into the mind at moments of leisure—while bathing, taking a walk, lying in a hammock, or driving to work—and they stun us with their brilliance, with their perfection. They are like one of nature's creatures, perfect in coloration and form. But they are just as wary, too. They can vanish as quickly as they came, to disappear into the incredible and labyrinthine forest of the mind. And they can become inextricably lost, never to be seen again.

I keep paper all over my house, and writing instruments. But what do you do with an idea that comes to you when you're washing your hair, covered with lather in the shower? In my car I have a battery-operated electronic secretary into which I can, in an instant, dictate an idea, a thought. On longer trips, I'll fill an entire cassette. People passing me in their cars see me talking into a small black device and no doubt think I'm a member of the CIA or some other arcane organization...or maybe just out of my mind.

But I have come to learn that ideas are the world's most valuable things. Ideas are the product of the human mind, the world's acknowledged winner in the "most valuable" category.

Ideas are a form of energy, and they need to be converted into something productive or useful, or interesting or entertaining, or, like more than 99.9 percent of the sun's rays, they will stream beyond into the endless void. And to stop and begin the conversion process, the idea must be translated into words, like radio signals, on a piece of paper. Then, the idea must be thought about, studied, and finally formed into physical reality. Everything we see about us was once an invisible idea. I remember thinking about that one time many years ago when I drove my car over the Oakland Bay Bridge connecting San Francisco and Oakland, California. What an incredible structure—and it began as an idea in the mind of a single human being.

People tend to underestimate their own ideas, simply because they have formed lifetime habits of underestimating themselves. Even in the top echelons of business there is a tendency to follow the other guy, because we tend to give the other guy credit for being smarter and more creative than we are.

And the experts tell us that most people don't get many ideas because they have never learned their importance nor the means of developing them.

To develop good ideas, one needs an active, inquiring, creative mind. She needs to develop the habit of questioning everything, realizing that nothing is as good as it will be and that we live in a state of constant change.

Ideas Alone
Aren't Enough

I RAN ACROSS A QUOTATION I LIKE. It reads, "Every time one man puts an idea across, he finds ten men who thought of it before he did—but they only thought of it."

There has never been a monopoly when it comes to getting good ideas, but the number of people who will take the raw material of a good idea and from it fashion reality in the world is small, indeed.

We have a tendency to think that when we get a good idea, we have to come up with something wholly new. And of course, this is quite possible. But the odds are that the same idea has flashed across the minds of many others—hundreds, perhaps thousands. And this is not important. An idea that remains only an idea and nothing more is of little or no value. It doesn't do anything and for all practical purposes might just as well have remained unborn.

It's true, as Victor Hugo put it, that "nothing in this world is so powerful as an idea whose time has come." And it's also true that there is nothing in this world of less value than an idea about which nothing is done.

People often write to large companies with unsolicited ideas, which, incidentally, most large companies wish they would not do. The same idea may have been suggested by others, including people within the company, for many years. Finally, let's say the company actually does something about the idea. It spends its brains, time, materials, and money to produce the product and immediately is deluged by angry letters, each claiming that the idea has been stolen and intimating that the company rose to its present prominence and success by stealing ideas from the helpless "little" people of the world.

It's a funny thing about people and their ideas. Most of the time the idea is the only thing the person is willing to risk. He'll risk that because it didn't cost anything. But ask him to back his faith in his idea with every nickel he can lay his hands on or borrow, and you often find his attitude undergoing a significant change.

This is a good test of ideas; it's also a good test of whether your idea is really the one you've been looking for—your big idea: if you're willing to stake everything you can scrape up and borrow on it, maybe it's a good idea.

Don't be too concerned with trying to come up with an idea nobody has thought of before. Here you're competing with millions. Instead, be concerned with taking an existing, already successful idea and building your good ideas on it. And don't get in too big a hurry. One of the hardest things to learn is how long it takes to become really, substantially, solidly successful. Ninety-nine times out of a hundred, it takes many years, even when the idea is great.

It is believed that the most fortunate people on earth are those who have found an idea that's bigger than they are, that fills their lives with constant interest, challenge, and struggle. It might be growing better tomatoes or kids, doing something for the under-privileged, painting, writing a book, or starting a new business. But there's nothing better than an idea we do something about.

If you find yourself running out of ideas and things in which you can find interest, bestir yourself. Go sit on a rocky ledge and think, or buy a book, or take a long walk. Don't desert the world of ideas, and don't be content with the ideas only. Do something about them.

TRANSFORMATIONAL LIVING

Do you keep a list of your ideas handy?

When was the last time you acted on them? Make it a goal to choose one idea a week or a month to investigate, improve, or act upon.

See if there are ways to build upon the original ideas you generate.

Chapter Five

Using Courage to Achieve Success

How to Live on Faith

MY OLD FRIEND, Dr. Harold Blake Walker of Evanston, sent me something some time back that I enjoyed tremendously and I think you will, too. He wrote, "We live by faith or we do not live at all. Either we venture or we vegetate. If we venture, we do so by faith, simply because we cannot know the end of anything at its beginning. We risk marriage on faith or we stay single. We prepare for a profession by faith or we give up before we start. By faith, we move mountains of opposition or we're stopped by molehills.

"Faith, however, is not often tranquil and steady. It ebbs and flows like the tides of the restless sea. Normally, like Browning's Bishop, we are forever exchanging a life of doubt diversified by faith for one of faith diversified by doubt. Yesterday we began the day with confident hope and trust in its promise. Last night, perhaps after a trying and troublesome day, we were beset by doubt and anxiety."

We grope and fumble in search of certainty, wishing we could escape the doubts that haunt us. The peril is that we shall cease groping on through our doubts and live only on our negations.

What we need, you and I, is faith strong enough to bear the burden of our doubts. No man ever drilled an oil well without being troubled by misgivings as the drill chewed downward toward producing structures. But only a fool would cease drilling halfway to the hoped-for pool. It was William Morris, the painter, who wrote, "I tell you, it's no joke to paint a portrait. Into the painting of every picture that's worth anything there comes a period of doubt and despair. The artist, however, goes on with his work, beyond his doubt, to creative achievement."

Faith enough to carry our doubts—it's enough. Perhaps it's all we can manage when fears assail and doubts annoy. Maybe we can do no more than grope on through our uncertainties, pursuing the enterprises of our lives in a grim trust that the end will justify the struggle.

If, despite our gnawing doubts, we can muster faith enough to take a single step on the road to where we're going, we are on the way to creative achievement. Every triumph of the human spirit begins with one step taken in faith. The single step is the small handle to great matters. No man or woman ever won a worthy triumph without fail to keep on and on, always able to last at least five minutes longer. There's one further thing to be said—namely, that worthy triumphs cannot be won without faith enough to maintain our integrity. One of the ultimate tests of faith is our capacity to go on believing that somehow the right is the right, even when right is on the scaffold and wrong seems to be on the throne.

All of the great ventures of our lives require faith enough to bear the burden of our doubts so that we're able to take the first step in the direction in which we wish to go—enough faith to keep on going through struggle and strain and to maintain integrity on the way. I like that. Yes, "faith is the assurance of things hoped for, the conviction of things not seen." And we need to exchange a life of doubt diversified by faith for a life of faith diversified by doubt.

What Do You Believe In?

It is what you believe in that will determine the course of your life, what happens to you and your ultimate destiny.

WHEN WAS THE LAST TIME you were asked the rather personal question: What do you believe in?

It sometimes seems that there is so much doubt, fear, and cynicism—so much tongue-in-cheek and wise-guy-elbow-rib-poking—that we have come to the place where people don't believe in anything anymore. People doubt their own capacity for judgment, for knowing what is right or wrong. They wait to see what others do or say before they'll express an opinion of their own. So what do you believe in?

This is not an unimportant question. It is vital that each of us decides exactly what he does believe in, and here's why: it is what you believe in that will determine the course of your life, what happens to you and your ultimate destiny. The great truth, "as you believe, so shall it be done unto you," seems to go almost unnoticed today, but that's the way it works. What you believe is what will happen to you. For belief is faith, and faith is still the greatest power on earth.

A young medical student was being examined by a board of distinguished doctors to determine whether or not he would receive his license to practice. They asked him, "Why do you want to be a physician?" and he replied, "I've known I was going to be a doctor for as long as I can remember. There is simply no question about it. I'm going to be a practicing physician and a good one."

He didn't beg the question. He told them he was going to be a doctor. They had no choice in the matter. The difference between faith and wanting, or wishing, is that with faith we know what is going to be, but with the others we are only hoping. It is what we believe that makes us the kind of people we are. The greater our faith, the greater we become. People who let others do their thinking for them, who will not venture forth an opinion on any subject until they're sure what they say will be met with approval and acceptance, do not believe. They conform to a picture of what they think others want them to be like. They are chameleons, ready to take on any hue their surroundings demand. They have no deep anchors of belief and drift aimlessly on the surface of life.

So, when asked, "What do you believe in?" it means "What do you have faith in? On what would you be willing to risk everything you have because of the certainty of your belief?"

If a person believes he is not much of a person, that's what he is. If he believes that he has value, that there is no other person on earth exactly like him, that he has an important contribution to make, and that he can reach the goals he sets for himself, these things are then true and will come to pass. People remain where they are because they believe that's where they ought to be, and they rise to new heights of achievement and ability because they believe they will.

The greatest teachers who ever lived are men whose minds soared far above those of their times. They said that according to our faith will it be done unto us. That, my friend, is the way it works. There are no arguments, no exceptions, no hair-splitting. What do you believe? Then that's what you are.

The worst thing that can happen to a person is to lose his belief in something. With belief gone, faith is gone, and when that's gone, there isn't anything left.

The Rewards
of Persistence

SOMETIMES IT APPEARS that there's a hidden guide someplace whose duty it is to test men and women through all sorts of discouraging experiences. Those who pick themselves up and keep trying after getting knocked down arrive. It's an uncanny thing, but it works. And this hidden guide lets no one enjoy great achievement without passing the persistence test, it seems. And those who can't take it simply don't make the grade.

And those who can take it are bountifully rewarded for their persistence. They receive as their compensation whatever goal they're pursuing. And that's not all, because they receive something infinitely more important than material compensation, although they get that. But they get the knowledge that every failure brings with it the seed of an equivalent advantage. There are exceptions to this rule. A few people know from experience the soundness of persistence. They're the ones who have not accepted defeat as being anything more than temporary. They're the ones whose desires are so persistently applied that defeat has finally changed into victory.

I was reading just the other day about the great Knute Rockne of Notre Dame who believed and applied this very thing we're talking about. He had a blood clot in one leg, and his doctors told him that if that blood clot traveled through his bloodstream to his heart, it would kill him. But the Notre Dame team was playing far from home that day, and he insisted on being taken to the game on a stretcher. So they got him to where the game was to be played. And they took him down to the dressing room where his football players were getting ready for the game. And the perspiration was running down his face and he was in terrible pain and he propped himself up on his elbows with a tremendous effort and said, "This team you're playing today beat us last year." And he said, "I want you to get out there and win." And it was then that he said, "The team that won't be beat, can't be beat." And then he fell back on his stretcher, out of breath and suffering terribly, and the team went out and won the game, and they never lost another game as long as Knute Rockne was alive, because when they saw the type of courage that he could develop, how persistently he fought to win even though he was flat on his back, it made giants out of men.

And people who stand on the sidelines of life see the overwhelmingly large number who go down in defeat, never to rise again. They see the few who take the punishment of defeat as an urge to greater effort. And these fortunately never learn to accept life's reverse gear. But what we don't see, what most of us never suspected existed, is the silent but irresistible power which comes to the rescue of those who fight on in the face of discouragement. Now if we speak of this power at all, we call it persistence and let it go at that. One thing we all know, if one does not possess persistence, one cannot achieve any noteworthy success in any calling.

TRANSFORMATIONAL LIVING

When was the last time you gave up without really trying?

When was the last time you persisted in spite of setbacks?

What did you learn from both experiences?

How to Free Your Mind from Fear

VIKTOR FRANKL, a distinguished psychiatrist and survivor of unspeakable atrocities at the hands of the Nazis in one of their concentration camps, says, "The last of the human freedoms is to choose one's attitude in any given set of circumstances." In fact, it was learning this that kept him free and alive even while he was languishing in a death camp.

Attitude, being an inner thing, can keep us free—even fairly cheerful—regardless of the environment in which circumstances may have placed us. The ancient philosophers had discovered this fact. But it seems that each maturing person must rediscover it for himself if he's to find his own brand of freedom.

Dr. Frankl also wrote, "Fear makes come true that which one is afraid of." Even if it only comes true in the imagination, we must experience the tortures of that which we fear—tortures that are, as often as not, worse than those that might actually come to pass in our lives. It's why the old line "A coward dies a thousand deaths; a brave man dies but once" is really true.

"Fear makes come true that which one is afraid of." If fear of something is held long enough, it may well bring on that which we fear. But it really doesn't make much difference, because experiencing the fear is the same thing—that is, as far as our mind and body are concerned, it's actually happening, over and over again, doing its inevitable damage to our physical bodies.

Ralph Waldo Emerson said that "fear is ignorance." Whenever we're afraid of something—I don't mean the perfectly natural, normal fears that work to keep us alive, but the gnawing, unreasoning, illogical, and neurotic fear of something—it's only because we don't know the real truth about it. If we did, the fear would vanish. That would include a neurotic fear of death, the fear that we are not liked or loved, and so forth.

I think the thing to remember here is that when we fear something, it takes its toll on our mind and body, just as if that which we fear had, in fact, come to pass. And we can bring to pass that which we fear, as Dr. Frankl said.

But how does a person change an attitude of fear? Dr. William Glasser, the distinguished psychiatrist and author of *Reality Therapy* and *Schools Without Failure* says, "If you want to change attitudes, start with a change in behavior." In other words, begin to act the part, as well as you can, of the person you would rather be, the person you most want to become. Gradually, the old fearful person will fade away.

Dr. Frankl learned that by controlling his attitude, the concentration camp fell away. His mind was free to roam where he wanted it to roam, think about what he wanted it to think about; it was as free as the birds—freer, really, for it could fly to the ends of the earth, to the ends of imagination, in an instant. And so can yours.

"The last of the human freedoms is to choose one's attitude in any given set of circumstances." We can let circumstances rule us, or we can take charge and rule our lives from within.

Give Yourself
the Gift of Courage

JUST AS I WAS BOARDING my plane in Sydney, Australia, to return to the United States, my old friend Roly Leopold of Melbourne handed me a small booklet. He said, "I think you'll enjoy reading this on the flight home."

The title of the little book was *The Gift of Courage*, written by Paul Speicher. Let me read a part to you:

"If you could have as a gift your dearest wish fulfilled, the wish that lies closest to your heart, the thing that you want most in the world, what would you choose? A million dollars? Abounding health? A magic solution to business worries? A content mind? A devoted family? The privilege of traveling only on the hilltops in the morning sun? Escape from the ills of life which are common to all?

"What gift would be more worthy of you than the fulfillment of an ideal daydream? What one thing would help you win through the problems you face today and may face again tomorrow? What gift would enable you to enjoy because you have fought, to rest because you have labored, to reap because you have sown?

"There is such a gift within your grasp, a gift which you yourself can give yourself, a gift which will bring all the things for which you secretly long, a gift which, like magic, will help clear the troubled roadway ahead and set your feet upon the pathway to real happiness.

"And that is the gift of courage."

Emerson wrote, "What a new face courage puts on everything!" And no truer statement was ever written. Whenever it appears, courage changes things for the better. Sometimes it's the courage to be silent when a word or phrase leaps to our mind. It's often the courage to get up on a cold, miserable morning, when it's the last thing in the world you want to do, to go to work. It's the courage to do what needs to be done when it should be done. It's the courage to discharge a person who should be discharged and who will probably be better off because of it. And it's the courage to follow the silent voice within you when it means going against the crowd or speaking out when you know what you're going to say will be unpopular with your listeners. It's the courage to stay with something long enough to succeed at it, realizing that it usually takes two, three, or four times as long to succeed as you first thought or hoped.

"There is such a gift within your grasp...a gift which, like magic, will help clear the troubled roadway ahead and set your feet upon the pathway to real happiness. And that is the gift of courage."

When Laughter Does More Harm Than Good

When our desire to belong to our crowd is more important to us than to stand up for what we know to be right, we have to admit that we are lacking in the two most important attributes of a human being—courage and maturity.

DO YOU KNOW WHAT FORM of punishment people dread more than any other? Well, it's laughter. That's right. As a wise man once wrote, "The deepest principle of human nature is the craving to be appreciated." And the exact opposite of being appreciated is to be laughed at. In fact, among the Eskimos, laughter is the only punishment for thieves. If the person is found to be a thief, all the Eskimos in the village laugh at him whenever they see him. As a result, there is very little stealing among Eskimos.

This is the reason youngsters in school like to dress alike. I drove by a corner the other day where four or five girls who looked to be of high school age were waiting for a school bus. They were all wearing identical coats. It appeared at first that they belonged to some kind of an organization that demanded that its members wear uniforms. Even though dressing like everyone else has the effect of removing our individuality and causing us to disappear by blending in with the crowd, it is much better than taking the risk of being laughed at. And since children will laugh more quickly at an individual who is different than will adults, children are much more conscious of wearing what all the other kids are wearing.

Laughter is the severest form of criticism, and the fear of criticism keeps us from doing a lot of things. It keeps us from doing a lot of things we should not do, and that's good, as laughter keeps Eskimos from stealing, but it also keeps us from doing a lot of things that we would be better off doing.

It is one of the enormous pressures of environment.

Take the worker, for example, who avoids doing an outstanding and conscientious job because the fear that his more cynical associates might laugh at him. Here, the fear of criticism in the form of laughter could shape a man's life and keep him from the goals and achievements he might otherwise reach if he weren't so conscious of how his actions will look to others. It is here that a better understanding of what is right and wrong can overcome a person's fear of criticism.

Frequently, being right and doing what is right can bring down upon us criticism and derision, while going along with things, even though we know they are wrong, will keep us "in good" with the crowd and our associates. And it is right here that the men are separated from the boys, the women from the girls. When our desire to belong to our crowd is more important to us than to stand up for what we know to be right, we have to admit that we are lacking in the two most important attributes of a human being—courage and maturity.

Winston Churchill once said, "Courage is the finest of human qualities because it guarantees all the others."

And if there is one vital aspect of living successfully that we should get across to our youngsters, it is this.

If our kids want to dress like all the other kids in their class, fine, that's normal—and we were the same way when we were kids. But they should be told why they want to look like all the other kids in school; that it is their natural desire to belong, to be liked; and that while that is perfectly alright, they should keep constantly in mind that it should end there—that it is also right that we should want to grow into individuals, with individual goals, individual thinking, individual action; and that we will be happiest if we will do our work as best as we possibly can, even though it may be the fashion for most of the rest to slide along as easily as possible.

F. D. Huntington wrote, "Conduct is the greatest profession. Behavior is the perpetual revealing of us. What a man does tells us what he is."

Learning to Fail through Effort, Not Fear

HERE'S A QUESTION FOR YOU: If you came across a plank on the ground—say the plank is twelve feet long, four inches thick, and twelve inches wide—you'd have no trouble walking from one end of it to the other. Now let's stretch that plank between two buildings that are one hundred feet tall. With nothing under you except one hundred feet of air and a street down below, would you walk the plank now? Same plank, same distance, but a different, more demanding situation.

And let's say you're telling your family, gathered around the dinner table, about something in which you believe very much—your philosophy of living, for example. Now change the setting to an auditorium; you're standing on the stage before a thousand people. How would you feel about making the talk now? You'd be saying the same thing, in the same way, but the setting has changed.

Walking the plank and making the talk are easy for you in one set of circumstances. Without changing your performance at all but changing the setting, a new element is introduced—one that alters your mental attitude considerably. That element is fear—fear of what might happen. Fear of what might happen under this new set of circumstances turns two perfectly simple and natural performances into occasions of great risk—so great that you might refuse to do either of them.

Since you know perfectly well that you can walk the plank when it's on the ground, it stands to reason that you can walk the same plank anywhere else. If you can make a talk under one set of circumstances, you can make the same talk under any other conditions. But fear seems to keep us from taking a formula we know will work under one condition and applying it to a large situation; the fear of what might happen holds us back.

We permit ourselves to fail by default rather than run the risk of failing as a result of having made the effort to succeed. Now, it's not important that we walk the length of the plank whether it's on the ground or high in the air. And it's not too important whether we make our little talk to the people in the auditorium, perhaps. But how many things are there at which we succeed at which we could be successful on a much larger scale? It's all a mental game. We play the whole thing out in our minds, and it's there—not in actual—that we win or lose.

No one can even guess how much is lost by the so-called average person simply because he fears to make the attempt. His fear of failure in his own eyes and in the eyes of his family and friends and the possible loss of a small stake raise a formidable wall between his reality and his dream. So he contents himself to peek at his dream over the top of the wall and wait—wait until conditions are better or until Uncle Charlie dies and leaves all that money. But waiting just seems to make the wall grow higher. Conditions seem to remain about the same, and Uncle Charlie is going to outlive everybody in the family. And finally, even on tiptoes, you can't see over the wall anymore. It's too high now, and it's too late. Well, so what? It was just an idea—a dream.

Yes, that's all it was—just an idea, a dream. But what could it have been? What might it have been if you'd scrambled over that wall before it got too high?

TRANSFORMATIONAL LIVING

What are some of the things you've avoided recently out of fear?

Choose one thing and promise yourself to do it anyway, in spite of your fear. If you fail, try again. What have you learned?

When to Keep Going
Even if You Don't Succeed

*When things start to look bleak, remember that you have the
power to change them and that you're the only creature
on earth with that kind of power.*

HERE'S A LINE WORTH REMEMBERING; it was written by
Balzac: "By resorting to self-resignation, the unfortunate consummate their misfortune."

There's a world of truth, and a world of unnecessary suffering,
in that statement. The only thing that can keep misfortune hang-
ing around is self-resignation—giving up. It makes you wonder how
many thousands—perhaps millions—of fine people stay on the bottom of the pile because they've formed the habit of saying, "Well,
that's the way things are" or "That's the way the old ball bounces."

Now, that would be all right for cows and pigs; they have to take
life as it comes. But it's the very thing a person does not have to do.
If things are going badly for him, he can change things and cause
them to become good. If he isn't making enough money, he can find
ways of earning more. If he doesn't like his neighborhood, he can
move. If he doesn't like his job, he can quit. If he doesn't like being
ignorant, he can get an education. He can, as a matter of fact, do
anything he wants to do. But as a rule, he doesn't know this. So he
shrugs his shoulders, gets a sad look on his face, stands still, does
nothing, and says, "Well, that's the way it is." If everybody had said

that from the very beginning, we'd still be running around without clothes on, throwing rocks at each other.

Let's go back to Balzac's little epigram. He said, "By resorting to self-resignation, the unfortunate consummate their misfortune." In other words, by wallowing in self-resignation, the unfortunate cause a bad situation to get worse and stay there.

Every human being on earth is going to suffer a setback from time to time. Setbacks are a part of life, as are fires, floods, tornadoes, hurricanes, and earthquakes. But fortunately, the human being is a builder and a rebuilder, and he rebuilds better than he builds. He doesn't sit in the aftermath of the storm and resign himself; he builds better next time so the damage won't be as great or even hurt him at all. This is how skyscrapers evolved from mud huts.

Outside of death and taxes, we don't have to resign ourselves to anything. And if the situation is bad, unfortunate, or unpleasant, self-resignation, as Balzac pointed out, will consummate the fact.

To my mind, there are few people to be pitied more than the sighers, resigners, and shoulder-shruggers—those who would rather complain than think, who would rather bleat than take action, who would rather ask for help than help themselves. If you know people like that, it's a good idea to keep away from them unless you're very strong. They'll infect you with their virus, splash you with their mud, and they're almost impossible to help. Like rag dolls, they'll flop right back down again the minute you turn loose of them. Just make sure you don't adopt any of the fatal habits.

When things start to look bleak, remember that you have the power to change them and that you're the only creature on earth with that kind of power. Build better and stronger next time. Do something about it; change a bad situation into a good one. Don't ask how; figure it out for yourself!

It has been written that "it is often better to have a great deal of harm," rather than a little, "happen to one. A great deal of harm may rouse you to remove what a little harm will only accustom you to endure."

Chapter Six

The Secret to Perseverance

The Flame of Hope

WHEN A CHILD IS BORN, he or she comes equipped with certain basic drives that psychologists have been listing for us for many years. And to my mind, one of the most interesting of these basic drives is the one we might call the drive to go on—the virtually indestructible tendency on the part of a human being to keep going, to wait for one more sunrise, to try just one more time and then once more again and again.

No matter how crushed, how defeated, how demoralized, when all hope seems gone, there is, in the healthy person, a small inextinguishable flame of hope—like a faint but persistent pilot light—that stays lit, much like the fire ancient man used to carry with him as he moved from place to place.

It's been seen in the faces of men, women, and children escaping from behind the Iron Curtain, and refugees from countries such as Vietnam, Cambodia, and Afghanistan. It was still smoldering in the shrunken faces of the victims of Hitler's death camps when they were liberated by the Allied soldiers at the close of World War II. It's what causes a person to keep putting one foot in front of the other on what seems like an endless road with no destination in sight. And it's this natural drive to go on, to keep trying, that's responsible for man's progress through the long centuries.

Almost everyone comes to a place in life when going on seems futile, even ridiculous—when he seems overwhelmed by a suffocating mattress of events and situations and desires just to sit down in the middle of the road and let the world and everything in it go to blazes.

So he sits down for a while. But then the vibration of the world seems to make itself felt to his bones. Pretty soon, he raises his head and begins to look around. After a while, he takes a couple of deep breaths; gets slowly, painfully, to his feet; wobbles there for a minute or two; and then he starts out again. As often as not, around the next bend in the road he'll find the reason he kept going. And he'll shudder at the thoughts of how close he came to giving up.

His hope lies in movement and time. If he doesn't get up and start moving again, he's done for. But he has this natural drive to keep moving along the road. As long as he keeps heading for what he's looking for, what seemed like the end of the world for him will be nothing more than a bad dream, and a part of the preparation he needed to qualify for the achievement his perseverance has brought.

Movement, time, and the law of averages. I remember reading about the manager of a Major League ball club who kept a rookie on the team and in the lineup because even though he wasn't hitting anywhere near what was expected of him, when he struck out, he struck out swinging. He wasn't just standing there watching strikes go by. And as the manager expected, he soon started getting wood on the ball and bringing his average up to where it belonged.

Discouragement seems to be a part of life, but the reason people prevail is because of this built-in drive to keep going.

The Cure for Procrastination

A person carrying a heavy weight is alright as long as he keeps moving. The minute he stops, puts the weight down on the ground, and sits down to rest, the weight seems to become heavier; the distance to be traveled, greater; and the work, just that much more unpleasant.

HAVE YOU EVER NOTICED that the longer you look at something you should be doing, the more difficult it seems to appear? That the longer you put off something you should do, the more difficult it is to get started?

A good deal of frustration and unhappiness could be avoided if people would just do what they know they should do.

The great newspaper editor Arthur Brisbane once wrote, "Don't exaggerate your own importance, your own size, or your own miseries. You are an ant in a human anthill. Be a working ant—not a ridiculous insect pitying yourself." Strong language, maybe, but there's a lot of sense in it.

A person carrying a heavy weight is alright as long as he keeps moving. The minute he stops, puts the weight on the ground, and sits down to rest, the weight seems to become heavier; the distance to be traveled, greater; and the work, just that much more unpleasant.

Sometimes it must seem to everyone that things have piled up so high there's just no way of digging out. But there is. Pick the thing that's most important to do, and simply begin doing it. Just by digging in, you'll feel better, and you'll find that it's not nearly as bad as you thought it would be. Keep at it, and before long, that pile of things to do that seemed so overwhelming is behind you, finished.

What overwhelms us is not the work itself. It's thinking how hard it's going to be. It's seeing it get larger every day. It's putting it off and hoping that somehow, through some miracle, it will disappear.

The Chinese have a saying that a journey of a thousand miles begins with but a single step. And that step accomplishes two things. First, it automatically shortens the distance we still have to travel, and second (and just as important), it makes us feel better, more hopeful—it strengthens our faith. And if a person will just keep putting one foot in front of the other, he will be taken into new and exciting places, see new and interesting things, and think thoughts that never would have come to him if he'd remained at the starting point. And then the journey is finished. He wonders how or why he could ever have sat so long and worried and stewed about the time and trouble it would involve to do what he knew he should do.

If you'll think back, you'll remember that you've always been happiest, most contented, after having finished a different project or faced up to a responsibility you were worried about. It's never so bad as you think it's going to be, and the joy that will come with its accomplishment makes it more than worthwhile.

Work never killed anyone. It's worry that does the damage. And the worry would disappear if we'd just settle down and do the work.

As Calvin Coolidge put it, "All growth depends upon activity. There is no development physically or intellectually without effort, and effort means work. Work is not a curse; it is the prerogative of intelligence, the only means to manhood, and the measure of civilization."

<hr />

Falling Isn't Failing

MARY PICKFORD USED TO SAY, "Don't look at the sudden loss of a habit or a way of life as the end of the road; see it instead as only a bend in the road that will open up all sorts of interesting possibilities and new experiences. After all, you've seen the scenery on the old road for so long, and you obviously no longer like it."

The breaking of a long-time habit does seem like the end of the road at the time—the complete cessation of enjoyment. Suddenly dropping the habit so fills our minds with the desire for the old habitual way that, for a while, it seems there will no longer be any peace, any sort of enjoyment. But that's not true. New habits form in a surprisingly short time, and a whole new world opens up to us.

For those who have tried repeatedly to break a habit of some kind only to repeatedly fail, Mary Pickford said, "Falling is not failing unless you fail to get up." Most people who finally win the battle over a habit they have wanted to change have done so only after repeated failures. And it's the same with most things.

So don't think of it as the end of the road but as a bend in the road. And falling is not failing unless we fail to get up again.

I remember in Arthur Miller's play *The Price*, the father lost everything during the stock market crash of 1928 and, for the rest of his life, sat in a room in the attic of a relative. That's failing. It seems some people lack the stamina, the energy, to do it all over again or to make a new start. For them, it's just the end of the road, and they've come to a full stop. Many lead such superficial lives, have so little depth of mind and spirit, that the sudden loss of income or material things is too much for them, and they jump out a window or retreat into insanity.

I remember hearing the story of the little boy who wanted to get over the backyard fence. He stood for a long time looking at the fence, and then slowly, with many falls and failures, he dragged a box to the fence. After many more attempts and falls, he managed to get to the top of the box. But he still couldn't reach the top of the fence. He set to work once again, this time getting a small box to place on the top of the big one. Again, he fell many times and had to get back on his feet. After much tugging, pushing, lifting, and dropping, he got the small box on top of the big box, laboriously clambered to the top of it, grasped the top of the fence, and flopped over.

So if you've been trying to start in a new direction, you might do well to remember the advice of Mary Pickford: It isn't the end of the road; it's just a bend in the road. And falling isn't failing unless you don't get up.

The Secret to Perseverance

MANY YEARS AGO, I discovered Professor William James's wonderful little book *On Vital Reserves*. In it, he says that everyone knows what it is to start a piece of work, either intellectual or physical, feeling stale. And everyone knows what it is to warm up to his work. The process of warming up is particularly striking in the phenomenon known as "second wind."

Now, usually, most people stop working at the first sign of fatigue. They say, "Boy, I'm bushed," and that's it for the day. As Dr. James put it, "We have then walked, played, or worked enough, so therefore we desist." We simply quit. This sort of fatigue forms a kind of wall inside of us. As a rule, we work and live our lives, but if an unusual necessity forces us to press onward, a surprising thing occurs: the fatigue gets worse up to a certain critical point; then gradually or suddenly it passes away, and we are fresher than before. We have evidently tapped a level of new energy that had until then been masked by the "fatigue barrier" we usually obey. In fact, we may have discovered that we have third and fourth winds.

The phenomenon occurs in mental activity as well as physical, and in some cases we may find, beyond the fatigue point, stores of energy that we never dreamed we possessed. Evidently, we stockpile reserves of energy we don't ordinarily use. And these reserves will go to work only when we demand enough of ourselves.

Only a few exceptional persons make any serious demands of themselves. The great majority of us miss the far greater accomplishments of which we are capable—and the greater joy in living this would bring to us—because we quit and sit down, gasping at the first sign of fatigue.

I remember one Sunday when I knew I had to write ten radio shows all in one day. I got started at nine o'clock in the morning and by five o'clock that afternoon I was so bushed I could hardly think. But I still had five shows to write, so I kept at it. All of a sudden, I felt better and had more energy than I had previously. And by 1:30 the next morning, when I finally finished, I felt great.

After sixteen and a half hours of steady mental work, I was as fresh as a daisy! But I had felt like quitting after only seven or eight hours.

The next time you get tired and you're doing something important, stay with it and see what happens. Each of us has a tremendous second wind, mental and physical. Passing through the fatigue barrier to draw upon our idle reserves can make the difference between existing and really living.

Emerson said, "Vigor is contagious; and whatever makes us either think or feel strongly adds to our power and enlarges our field of action."

The Value of Active Patience

Every time a person admits to himself—usually much later—that he has made a fool of himself, he can trace it to a lack of patience. If he had only waited awhile, everything would have been alright.

TO A CHILD, waiting five minutes for the motion picture to begin or counting the minutes until the family arrives at grandmother's house can seem like an eternity. To talk to children in terms of months, to say nothing of years, is to boggle their impatient little minds.

But as the years pass, a good measure of maturity can be said to be the degree of a person's patience. And the older and, hopefully, wiser a person becomes, the more he comes to realize the importance of patience. He learns that it's a little short of amazing when it comes to the size and number of problems that can be solved by the passage of time.

It's as though everyone is riding on the outer edge of a great wheel that turns very slowly but that will, in time, bring everyone to his turn of great good fortune, if he's doing things right.

Often, crimes of violence can be traced to nothing more than a lack of patience. And the number of broken marriages that could be heaped upon this same cause must number in the many millions. And how many times do parents later wish they had not acted or spoken so quickly at something their child had done?

Every time a person admits to himself—usually much later—that he has made a fool of himself, he can trace it to a lack of patience. If he had only waited awhile, everything would have been alright.

It's been said that everything comes if a person will only wait. And it was Benjamin Franklin who said, "He that can have patience can have what he will." And Horace Bushnell wrote, "It is not necessary for all men to be great in action. The greatest and most sublime power is often simple patience." And de Maistre said, "To know how to wait is the great secret of success." Not to leave out Shakespeare, who wrote, "How poor are they who have not patience! What wound did ever heal but by degrees."

But patience is not passive and should never be confused with idleness and a phlegmatic insensibility. On the contrary, it is active, it is concentrated strength, it is perseverance—it is knowing that to persevere is to prevail.

Aristotle wrote that "patience is so like fortitude that she seems either her sister or her daughter." And Rousseau said, "Patience is bitter, but its fruit is sweet."

A great life, a great home and family, a great career, a great business, a great accomplishment of any kind—all these come with patience—patience with others, with the world, and with ourselves.

It is said that every day begins a new year for each of us. If you're in the mood for a little self-improvement, for turning over a new leaf, write the word *patience* some place where you'll see it every day for the next, oh, say, fifty or sixty years. You'll be amazed what this one word can do for your life.

There is as much difference between genuine patience and sullen endurance as there is between the smile of love and the malicious gnash of teeth. If your turn has not yet come, keep at it, and be patient.

———◆◆◆———

Chapter Seven

MANAGING RISK IN YOUR LIFE

Look for Opportunity, Not Security

THE STOIC PHILOSOPHER EPICTETUS taught, "Adversity introduces a person to himself. On the occasion of every accident that befalls you, remember to turn to yourself and inquire what power you have for turning it to use.

"Opportunity beckons more surely when misfortune comes upon a person than it ever does when that person is riding the crest of a wave of success. It sharpens a person's wits, if he will let it, enabling him to see more clearly and evaluate his situation with a more knowledgeable judgment."

It's been my observation that people seem to be growing more and more fearful of risk of any kind. They seem bent on an almost frantic scramble for security without taking the time to think it all the way through.

There's only one form of security we can attain during our lives. It's inner security—the kind that comes from courage, experience, and the ability and willingness to learn, to grow, to attempt the unknown. Security isn't what the wise person looks for; it's opportunity. And once we begin looking for that, we find it on every side. You can measure opportunity with the same yardstick that measures the risk involved. They go together.

The famous World War II admiral, William "Bull" Halsey, said, "Touch a thistle timidly, and it pricks you; grasp it boldly, and its spines crumble. All problems become smaller if you don't dodge them but confront them." I think we all know that, but we tend to forget it between problems.

I particularly like Epictetus's line: "Adversity introduces a person to himself." That's when we get to really know ourselves; that's when we come face to face with the real person we are and the stage of our maturity or growth to that point.

It does no good at all to worry about times in the past when we've failed to measure up in our own eyes. We weren't ready yet. We hadn't, at that point in our lives, matured sufficiently. We weren't wise enough. Besides, that's in the past. It's how we stand up to trouble now that matters. And we should keep in mind the truth and wisdom contained in his advice, "Opportunity beckons more surely when misfortune comes upon a person than it ever does when that person is riding the crest of a wave of success."

Most very successful people can remember that their success was discovered and built out of adversity of some kind. It's not the problems that beset us—problems are surprisingly pretty much the same for millions of others; it's how we react to problems that determines not only our degree of growth and maturity but our future success—and, perhaps, much of our health.

It's good to get rid of that word *security* once and for all. It makes us feel free again, as we felt as children, and we begin to see what this business of living is all about. We begin to really enjoy it.

Innovators and Risk-Taking

PEOPLE WHO DO WELL in the world by being creative and willing to take a calculated risk are people who manage to overcome the fear of laughter. Any time you attempt anything in which you risk failure, you run the risk of having people laugh at you. A college professor worked many years on an invention. He tramped all over New England trying to attract capital for his device for making the human voice travel along a wire. The people laughed at him. It was, of course, plumb idiotic, they said, to suppose that the human voice could be carried along a wire and heard for many miles, or even for a single mile. But our old friend and benefactor Alexander Graham Bell could not be laughed out of it. And every time we pick up the telephone we salute the man who stayed on course despite the laughter.

Millions of people laughing in derision could not hurt us an iota, but we stand in mortal terror of it. Men and women who can prove themselves heroes in great crisis tremble before derision. It's a queer quirk of human nature we probably develop as children. It has cost much. It has changed the history of the world.

Sometimes the price of a laugh has met the slamming of a door to fame and fortune, or even immortality.

Elias Howe invented the sewing machine, but it nearly rusted away before American women stopped laughing about it and could be persuaded to make use of it. "With their sewing done so quickly, they argued, what would they ever do with all their spare time?"— so a biographer paints a tragic picture. The man who had done more than any other to lighten the work of women was forced to borrow a suit of clothes on an occasion of a public appearance.

Men are as bad as women when it comes to resisting new ideas. The typewriter had been a demonstrated success for years before businessmen could be persuaded to buy it. "How could anyone have enough letters to write," they argued, "to justify the investment of $100 in a writing machine?"

Only when the Remingtons sold patent rights to the Caligraph Company and two groups of salesmen worked in competition was the resistance finally broken down. Xerography faced the same kind of problem when it was first introduced, and other inventions have had similar battles.

Here's an extract from a notebook of Robert Fulton, who invented the steamship, which changed the world from sail to steam. He wrote, "As I had occasioned daily to pass to and from the shipyard where my boat was in progress, I often loitered near the groups of strangers and heard various remarks as to the object of this new vehicle. The language was uniformly that of scorn, sneer, or ridicule. The loud laugh often rose at my expense. The dry jest, the wise calculations of losses or expenditures, the dull repetition of Fulton's folly. Never did a single encouraging remark, a bright hope, or a warm wish cross my path." And that's about what you can expect when you try something new.

Perversity and built-in envy cause people to think or hope that any new idea or plan that runs counter to established principle will fail. Emerson wrote, "Pythagoras was misunderstood, and Socrates and Jesus and Luther and Copernicus and Galileo and Newton and every pure and wise spirit that ever took flesh. To be great is to be misunderstood."

You know we tend to forget that the greatest people, the greatest writers, the greatest teachers were for the most part in violent disagreement with their times and the way things were being done. We seem to have become so flabby in our acceptance of anything that we fail to do anything personally about what we see about us.

Norman Cousins wrote that the biggest issue of all in all the years ahead is not just the squandering of physical resources, but the squandering of human resources.

So what is failure? Failure does not come to a person because he is not recognized by the multitudes during his lifetime or ever. Our success or failure has nothing to do with the opinions of others. It has only to do with our own opinion of ourselves and what we're doing.

The only person that can be called a failure is that person who tries to succeed at nothing. Success, as far as a person is concerned, does not lie in achievement. It lies in striving, reaching, attempting.

Any person who decides upon a course of action he deems to be worthy of himself and sets out to accomplish that goal is a success right then and there.

TRANSFORMATIONAL LIVING

Think about some of the accomplishments you have made in your life. Have you taken your achievements for granted?

Have you done what you set out to do, in spite of the consequences?

Do you give up too quickly?

Reassess those things that were not successful for you and determine whether they are worth a second chance.

Playing It Safe Can Be Risky

In all walks of life, the most successful people are the risk-takers. They take the risk of being different when they believe in something. This has a tendency to make the going a little tougher for a while, but they almost always wind up ahead of the game eventually.

PEOPLE WHO PLAY IT TOO SAFE take the greatest risks. Did you know that? In the long haul, the intelligent risk-takers develop the greatest security. It's a wise person who learns the importance of risk-taking.

During World War II, psychologist Ellis Paul Torrance made a study of United States aces flying in the Pacific theater of operations. He reported that the most salient characteristic of the ace was his risk-taking ability. Throughout his life, he had kept testing the limits of his abilities. And the life histories of these men showed that they were highly resistant to accidents, and in combat they suffered fewer casualties than pilots who were inclined to play it safe. Dr. Torrance said "Living itself is a risky business. If we spent half as much time learning how to take risks as we spent avoiding them, we wouldn't have nearly so much to fear in life."

In all walks of life, the most successful people are the risk-takers. By that, I mean they risk believing in their own ideas, striking out toward their own goals, standing up for what they believe to be right. They take the risk of being different when they believe in something. This has a tendency to make the going a little tougher for a while, but they almost always wind up ahead of the game eventually.

Risk-takers realize there's nothing wrong with an occasional failure. The play-it-safers seem to think a failure means the end of the world.

The risk-takers are not foolhardy. Getting back to the World War II aces for a moment, it was found that these men were very fussy about their airplanes, armament, and equipment. They were painstaking in preparation and highly disciplined in following instructions and what they had been taught. But in an encounter with the enemy, they would immediately take charge and go on the offense. The best defense is often a good offense. The best defense in football is to rush the quarterback. When a storm comes up, ships in the harbor head for the raging open sea unless they're protected in slips. In the harbor, they could drag their anchors and wind up on the beach or the breakwater.

So what appears to be risk-taking is often the most intelligent course to follow. It leads to security, while what would appear to be the safest course of action can lead to disaster or, simply, nowhere.

A young woman whose romance had gone on the rocks told her mother that she was never going to permit herself to fall in love again. "You only get hurt," she said. "And if you don't fall in love," her mother said, "you don't live." It's another one of those risks the successful person is willing to take.

Everyone runs risks—quite sizable risks—every day of his life—risks he takes for granted or isn't even aware of. But when an unusual situation comes along that involves risk-taking, how do you decide whether or not to go ahead?

When a situation comes along that involves risk and you don't know whether to go ahead or hold back, reassess your goals. What are you trying to accomplish? What are you working toward? Will taking this risk, if it works out successfully, help you toward your goals?

✦

Advice for the Fearful

DR. JOYCE BROTHERS has some good advice for the fearful. She points out that everyone is familiar with fear. Normal fear protects us and provides a warning signal indicating the presence of danger. A totally fearless person is probably not too intelligent and can look forward to a very short life. But when fear is inappropriate, it can stand in the way of progress and success. It can destroy love, create failure on the job, and interfere with our ability to relate well to others.

Innovation and creativity involve risk, Dr. Brothers goes onto say. The person who's afraid to take chances, who's afraid of failure, is standing in the way of his progress.

In fact, an emotionally healthy person needs challenge in life. Studies show that people who are cautious in the extreme, who are afraid to take risks even when the odds are in their favor, tend to be afraid of life itself—which, of course, is also a gamble. Such persons are not likely to succeed in business or anything else.

Dr. Brothers suggests that such people practice failure. How liberating it would be for the average person to be able to walk into a room, trip over a wastebasket, have all the people in the office laugh, and then be able to laugh with them!

Dr. Brothers suggests that fearful people deliberately do such things to discover that an occasional failure is no disgrace but rather a perfectly normal part of living.

I remember when I was just starting out in radio, I managed to get the part of Sky King, the lead in the famous children's radio program of that name. And I would often be asked to make public appearances for schoolchildren. One day, I flew up to Michigan to greet and sign autographs for several hundred children allowed out of school for the event.

I flew there in a small two-seater airplane. I was dressed in my cowboy costume from my hat to my cowboy boots, gun belt—the works. As I was trying to climb out of the airplane cockpit in my unaccustomed costume, while the hundreds of children waited nearby, I caught my heel on the cockpit coaming and fell full-length on the wing. Then I did a slow roll off the trailing edge of the wing to the ground. My guns fell out, my hat rolled away, and a deathlike silence fell on the children. There was their hero, sprawled on the grass! He couldn't even get out of an airplane!

I picked up my guns, put my hat back on, and, with a sheepish grin from ear to ear, walked to the waiting children. We all had a good laugh about it, and I signed the autographs, and all went surprisingly well. As I flew back to Chicago, I thought about how often children fall and that they could easily empathize with me.

Don't lose your sense of humor, and remember that even though they may laugh, people are kinder and more forgiving than we generally give them credit for being. Risks and pratfalls are part of life; so is an occasional failure in other ways. And so is success—lots of it.

Chapter Eight

IMPROVING YOUR
ABILITY TO COPE

How to React to Stress

TWO YOUNG BOYS WERE RAISED by an alcoholic father. As they grew older, they moved away from that broken home, each going his own way in the world. Several years later, they happened to be interviewed separately by a psychologist who was analyzing the effects of drunkenness on children in broken homes. His research revealed that the two men were strikingly different from each other. One was a clean-living teetotaler, the other a hopeless drunk like his father. The psychologist asked each of them why he developed the way he did, and each gave an identical answer: "What else would you expect when you have a father like mine?"

That story was revealed by Dr. Hans Selye, internationally renowned Canadian physician and scientist known as the "father of stress." A medical pioneer, he devoted the majority of his years to the exploration of biological stress. And he related the story of the two sons of the drunken father in an article for *New Realities*. And the story demonstrates a cardinal rule implicit in stress, health, and human behavior. According to R. H. Schuller, "It is not what happens to you in life that makes the difference. It is how you react to each circumstance you encounter that determines the result. Every human being in the same situation has the possibilities of choosing how he will react—either positively or negatively."

Thus, stress is not necessarily caused by stressor agents; rather, it is caused by the way stressor agents are perceived, interpreted, or appraised in each individual case. Outside events and people upset some more than others, because they are looked upon and dealt with in entirely different ways. The stressors may even be the same in each case, yet the reaction will almost always be different in different people.

So what is the cause of our stress? The outside agents and people or the perception and interpretation each person brings to a given situation? If a microbe is in or around us all the time and yet causes no disease until we are exposed to stress, what is the cause of our illness—the microbe or the stress?

Basowitz, Persky, Korchin, and Grinker, in their book *Anxiety and Stress*, have this to say about the cause of stress: "The stress accruing from a situation is based...on the way the affected subject perceives it; perception depends upon the multiplicity of factors, including the genetic equipment, basic individual needs and longings, earlier conditioning influences and a host of life experiences and cultural pressures. No one of these can be singled out for exclusive emphasis. The common denominator of 'stress disorders' is reaction to circumstances of threatening significance to the organism."

Armed with that information, it would seem that we can greatly improve our reactions to stressful situations. What seems to be a cruel world to one person might be filled with challenge and opportunity to another. It is our reaction that makes the difference.

Only 8 Percent of Worries Are Worth It

ACCORDING TO THE BUREAU OF STANDARDS, "A dense fog covering seven city blocks, to a depth of 100 feet, is composed of something less than one glass of water." That is, all the fog covering seven city blocks, at 100 feet deep, could be, if it were gotten all together, held in a single drinking glass. It would not quite fill it. And this could be compared to our worries. If we can see into the future and if we could see our problems in their true light, they wouldn't tend to blind us to the world, to living itself, but instead could be relegated to their true size and place. And if all the things most people worry about were reduced to their true size, you could probably put them all into a water glass, too.

It's a well-established fact that as we get older, we worry less. We learn, with the passing of the years and the problems each of them yields, that most of our worries are not really worth bothering ourselves about too much and that we can manage to solve the important ones.

But to younger people, they often find their lives obscured by the fog of worry. Yet here's an authoritative estimate of what most people worry about: things that never happen, 40 percent—that is, 40 percent of the things you worry about will never occur anyway; things over and past that can't be changed by all the worry in the world, 30 percent; needless worries about our health, 12 percent; petty, miscellaneous worries, 10 percent; real, legitimate worries, 8 percent. Only 8 percent of your worries are worth concerning yourself about. Ninety-two percent are pure fog with no substance at all.

The wife or husband will nurse and cling to things that have happened or have been said in the past and keep exhuming them like desiccated corpses. If the collection gets large enough—and it could easily get large enough in even the best of households—if a person never forgets every little slight or oversight or word spoken in impatience or anger, the marriage will wind up on the rocks.

The largest cause of all arguments in the home, incidentally, is worry about money. And this wouldn't be such a problem—in fact, it could be a source of gratification—if we could just learn to live within our means and save a part of every dollar we earn. It isn't easy, but it will get rid of the worries and most of the argument about money. Ben Franklin said there are two ways of solving money problems: augment your means—that is, make more money—or diminish your wants. Either will do. But the best plan of all is to do both at the same time. Think of ways to earn more money and diminish your wants. In this way, you'll live well within your means and always have a nice surplus of money.

Nurture Your Ability to Laugh

I have found it a good rule of thumb to be slightly suspicious of anyone who takes himself too seriously. There's usually something fishy there someplace.

ONE OF THE ENRICHING BLESSINGS of growing older all the time is that it has a way of improving one's sense of humor—or at least it should. The person without a good sense of humor is a person to avoid as though he were a known carrier of a plague.

Horace Walpole once said, "I have never yet seen or heard anything serious that was not ridiculous." And Samuel Butler said, "The one serious conviction that a man should have is that nothing is to be taken seriously." It has been said that "seriousness is the only refuge of the shallow." Oscar Wilde said, "It is a curious fact that the worst work is always done with the best intentions and that people are never so trivial as when they take themselves very seriously."

I remember that when I was in the service, one of the toughest jobs I had was to keep from laughing at the wrong times—during an admiral's inspection, for example. There is nothing funnier than the seriousness of the military, especially high-ranking military. The fancy costumes, the panoply, the shining sabers, the serious faces—it was all, to me, hilariously funny.

We can be serious about situations. When a youngster is ill or hurt or someone insults your spouse, you can get very serious about the situation in a hurry. But that's not taking ourselves seriously. That's different.

The thing that bothered me about Hemingway, as much as I admired his work, was that I thought he tended to take himself too seriously. He didn't seem to be able to laugh at himself. And I think he suffered from this flaw in his character.

I have found it a good rule of thumb to be slightly suspicious of anyone who takes himself too seriously. There's usually something fishy there someplace. I think this is why we love children so much—life is a game to them. They will do their best at whatever work is given to them, but they never seem to lose their ebullient sense of humor; there is always a sparkle of humor in their eyes. When a child lacks this, he is usually in need of help.

Dictators are famous for their lack of humor. The mark of a cruel person is that he doesn't seem to be able to see anything funny in the world. And a sense of humor was what was so great about Mark Twain. No matter how serious the subject, he could find the humor in it and bring it out. So could Will Rogers. All the great comedians have this ability to see what's funny in the so-called serious situation. They can poke fun at themselves. There are those who believe that a sense of humor is the only thing that has kept the human race from totally extinguishing itself.

People who are emotionally healthy with a sense of proportion are cheerful people. They tend to look upon the bright side of things and see a lot of humor in their daily lives. They're not Pollyannas; they know what's going on and that a lot of it's not at all funny, but they don't permit the dark side of things to dominate their lives. To my mind, when a person lacks a sense of humor, there's something pretty seriously wrong with him.

Samuel Butler said, "A sense of humor keen enough to show a man his own absurdities as well as those of other people will keep a man from the commission of all sins, or nearly all, save those that are worth committing." It took a sense of humor to write that, and only people with blank spaces where their senses of humor should be will find it offensive. There's something so healthy about laughter, especially when it's directed at ourselves. This form of humor was what made Jack Benny and Bob Hope such durable and successful comedians, along with many others going clear back to Charlie Chaplin.

I remember the wonderful ending to that really fine motion picture, *The Treasure of Sierra Madre.* After months of back-breaking toil and the constant danger of death from bandits, the characters find they have lost all the gold and that they're right back where they started from. And suddenly they begin to laugh. They almost faint from laughter. And you realize they've seen themselves in their true perspective—the ludicrousness of the situation and their former greed. And just as suddenly, you realize that everything is all right again as they part and go their separate ways.

There are times of seriousness for all of us when all the laughter seems to be gone, but we should not permit these periods to last too long. When we've lost our sense of humor, there isn't very much left. We become ridiculous. We must then go to war against the whole world, and that's a war we've got to lose.

The Twelve Things to Remember

HERE ARE TWELVE THINGS TO REMEMBER. The author is unknown.

1. The value of time;

2. The success of perseverance;

3. The pleasure of working;

4. The dignity of simplicity;

5. The worth of character;

6. The power of example;

7. The influence of life;

8. The obligation of duty;

9. The wisdom of economy;

10. **The virtue of patience;**

11. **The improvement of talent; and**

12. **The joy of originating.**

Good list, isn't it? It could be the kind of checklist that a person might carry with him to glance at from time to time. None of us is smart enough to remember all he knows, as Will Rogers once said. We all need reminding.

The value of time. At first you might think that applies to working, which it does for part of the time, but it also applies to time spent not working—time spent thinking, or dreaming, or relaxing, or reading, or walking, or indulging in a favorite hobby. The value of time...not to waste it on things that do nothing to help or bring enjoyment.

The success of perseverance. Perseverance can accomplish anything. My friend W. Clement Stone tells the story of Tom, who was born without half of a right foot and only a stub of a right arm. As a boy, he wanted to engage in sports as the other boys did. He had a burning desire to play football, of all things. Because of this desire, his parents had an artificial foot made for him. It was made of wood. The wooden foot was encased in a special stubby football shoe. Hour after hour, day after day, he would practice kicking the football with his wooden foot. He would try, and keep on trying, to make field goals from greater and greater distances. He became so proficient that he was hired by the New Orleans Saints. Now, just offhand, what would you say a person's chances of playing professional football were if he were born without half of a right foot and a withered arm? But the screams of 66,910 football fans would be heard throughout the entire United States when Tom Dempsey, with his crippled leg, kicked the longest field goal ever kicked in a professional football game, within the last two seconds of the game, to give the Saints a winning score of nineteen to seventeen over the Detroit Lions. "We were beaten by a miracle," said Detroit coach Joseph Schmidt. But they were beaten by perseverance.

The pleasure of working. Often the pleasure that comes from working only comes after the work has been finished, but it's pleasure you can't find any other way.

The dignity of simplicity. If only more people could learn to keep things simple...straightforward...honest. It's best in everything from architecture to living.

The worth of character goes without saying. It is the one thing each of us can build for himself that gives value to his life and himself.

The power of example. The example set by parents will have a much greater influence on the life of a child than all the schooling in the world. The secret is, don't tell him; show him.

The obligation of duty gives meaning to our lives.

The wisdom of economy. This ties in with the dignity of simplicity.

The virtue of patience. Half the problems of the world could be prevented by patience. Give it a little time, and it will usually come out fine.

The improvement of talent. That's how we grow and mature at whatever we have chosen of our own free will to do with our lives.

And *the joy of originating.*

Great list—twelve things to remember.

A Short Memory Is Good and Bad

EVERYTHING IN NATURE HAS TWO SIDES: a good and a bad, a positive and a negative. In philosophy, this message goes back thousands of years to the Chinese yin and yang. The yang is the good—the sunny side of the hill; and the yin is the dark side. There is a dualism in everything in the universe. The rain that waters and fertilizes the crops also brings floods; the fire that warms our homes and cooks our meals causes widespread havoc when it's out of control.

And have you ever thought about the good and the bad sides of memory?

Each of us really has a very short memory. Sure, the subconscious remembers everything, but our conscious minds forget. We forget the bad, and that's good. We forget our failures, our mistakes, our foolishness, the pain we've caused, the opportunities we've missed, the love we've failed to give when it was needed. These things pass from our conscious memory as though from a filter to which they cling for a while and then are cleansed away by time.

But we also forget, to our pain, the good, and that's bad. We forget the principles, the systems which, if we will but live by them daily, will result in our achieving the things we want to achieve. We literally forget how to live successfully.

If, through some diabolical device, we were constantly reminded of all of our past failures and mistakes, we would live in a state of constant depression, fear, and sorrow—a hell on earth. But instead, our conveniently forgetful minds save us from this.

But if, through some wonderful agency, we could be constantly reminded only of the good, of those principles and systems that we know work to our benefit and the benefit of society, we would live in a state of optimism, enthusiasm, and hope. We would go from one success to another.

Well, it's a fact that the world's most successful people manage to accomplish this latter state. They manage to arrange their minds so that they constantly remind themselves of what they're doing and where they're going. They know for certain that if they'll just do certain things in a certain way every day, they will be led to the goals toward which they're striving.

Most news seems to be bad. Our newspapers and newscasts are not filled with all the good that's going on in the world. That would be kind of silly, I suppose. They report all the news, and the great majority of it seems to be on the negative side: wars, murders, crime, disasters, accidents, swindles, scandals. Additionally, most people are so constituted, or so lacking in the proper education, that they, too, seem to act and talk rather on the negative side, and we're influenced by them. If we live then in accordance with our environment, we'll tend to forget the good and dwell on the bad the majority of the time. This means we will live most of our lives on the dark side of the ancient Chinese hill.

What's the solution?

It is to find a way to remind ourselves every day, as do the really successful, of those things that lead to success, to the good. Otherwise, we'll forget the good along with the bad.

A Definition of the Self-Actualized Person

WHAT WOULD IT BE LIKE to be a fully mature, self-actualizing, fully functioning human being? This is the ideal, busy, happy person with all his faculties smoothly functioning in perfect cooperation—no wars going on inside, no hang-ups, no neuroses... the ideal, productive person.

Dr. Abraham Maslow has made a study of self-actualized people, and they stack up this way:

First, these superior people have the ability to see life clearly, to see it as it is rather than as they wish it to be. They are less emotional and more objective about their observations. They are far above average in their ability to judge people correctly and to see through the phony or the fake. Usually, their choice of marriage partners is far better than average, although by no means perfect.

These self-actualized people are more accurate in their prediction of future events. They see more fully, and their judgment extends to an understanding of art, music, politics, and philosophy.

Yet they have a kind of humility—the ability to listen carefully to others, to admit they don't know everything and that others can teach them. This concept can be described as a childlike simplicity and lack of arrogance. Children have this ability to hear without preconception or earthly judgment. As the child looks out upon the world with wide, uncritical, innocent eyes, simply noting or observing that is the case, without either arguing the matter or demanding that it be otherwise, so does the self-actualizing person look upon human nature in himself and in others.

Without exception, Maslow found self-actualizing people to be dedicated to some work, task, duty, or vocation that they considered important. Because they were interested in this work, they worked hard, and yet the usual distinction between work and play became blurred. For them, work is exciting and pleasurable.

Maslow found creativity to be a universal characteristic of all the self-actualizing people he studied. Creativeness was almost synonymous with the terms *healthy*, *self-actualizing*, and *fully human*.

Here again, the creativity of these people is similar to that of little children before they have learned to fear the ridicule of others. Maslow believes this to be a characteristic that is too frequently lost as we grow older. Self-actualizing people either do not lose this fresh naïve approach, or if they lose it, they recover it later in life.

Spontaneity is typical of this person. Self-actualizing people are less inhibited and therefore more expressive, natural, and simple. And of course, they have courage. The courage that is needed in the lonely moments of creation. This is a kind of daring, a going out in front all alone, a defiance, a challenge. Thus, while these persons are humble in that they are open to new ideas, they are willing to forego popularity to stand up for a new idea.

The self-actualizing person has a low degree of self-conflict. He is not at war with himself; his personality is integrated. This gives him more energy for productive purposes. As Maslow puts it, "Truth, goodness and beauty are in the average person in our culture only fairly well correlated with each other, and in the neurotic person even less so. It is only in the evolved and mature human being, in the self-actualizing, fully functioning person, that they are so highly corelated that for all practical purposes they may be said to fuse into a unity."

Research indicates that the healthy person is most integrated when facing a great creative challenge, some worthwhile goal, or a time of serious threat or emergency.

The psychologically healthy person is both selfish and unselfish, and in fact, these two attitudes merge into one. The healthy person finds happiness in helping others. Thus, for him, unselfishness is selfish. They get selfish pleasures from the pleasures of other people, which is a way of being unselfish. Or, saying it another way, the healthy person is selfish in a healthy way, a way that is beneficial to him and to society, too.

TRANSFORMATIONAL LIVING

What are the qualities of a
self-actualized person? They possess:

- *the ability to see life clearly,*

- *a childlike simplicity and lack of arrogance,*

- *dedication to some work that they consider important,*

- *the creativity of children,*

- *spontaneity and courage,*

- *a low degree of self-conflict,*

- *and both selfishness and unselfishness.*

Learning to
See with the Soul

ONE OF THE MAJOR TRAGEDIES of growing up is that the majority of us lose that wonderful capacity of children to see emotionally. Do you remember how you saw things when you were a small child? Sometimes things—and quite often the simplest—seemed so beautiful to us it was almost unbearable. That's why a small child, still unspoiled by the acquisitiveness of modern society, will keep the box or wrapping paper and throw away the gift.

I was fortunate to live a part of my childhood on a small farm in Northern California. It was beautiful country, and I can remember how the earth smelled after a rain and how unutterably beautiful everything was: the trees, the grass, the poppies, the sky, the clouds, the birds, the puddles of water in the dirt road. Every walk in the fields or woods was the greatest kind of adventure filled with beauty.

Well, I was reading W. H. Hudson—probably the greatest naturalist of his time—and came across this line: "We may say that the impressions are vivid and live vividly in the mind, even to the end of life, in those alone in whom something that is of the child survives in the adult—the measureless delight in all this visible world, experienced every day by the millions of children happily born outside the city's gates; and with the delight, the sense of wonder in all life, which is also akin to, if not one with, the mythical faculty, and if experienced in a high degree is a sense of the supernatural in all natural things. We may say, in fact that unless the soul goes out to meet what we see, we do not see it; nothing do we see—not a beetle, not a blade of grass."

That's why two people can look at the same sight and while one is transformed and struck dumb by the awesome beauty of it, the other person will turn and walk away. And the fact is, the other person didn't see it. He looked, but he didn't see it.

I remember coming back from Europe by ship one time, and one morning I came on deck to see the most beautiful and magnificent island I had ever seen. It was São Miguel, in the eastern Azores. I stood at the rail transformed by its sudden beauty for several minutes, then rushed below to bring my wife and son to see it. They thought it was beautiful too, but I could tell they had not been affected by it as I had. In the case of something else, things could very likely be reversed. But when we see, as Hudson says, somehow with the soul, "unless the soul goes out to meet what we see, we do not see it."

What makes an artist great (a writer, painter, or musician) is that in his work he is able, through some transcendent magic, to make things so real to us we are able to see them in that way—with our souls going out to them. It's very difficult to express, but anyone who's been a child can usually remember the wonderful way things appeared. The trick and the idea is to keep that faculty alive.

EARL NIGHTINGALE'S
BIOGRAPHY

AS A DEPRESSION-ERA CHILD, Earl Nightingale was hungry for knowledge. From the time he was a young boy, he would frequent the Long Beach Public Library in New York, searching for the answer to the question, "How can a person, starting from scratch, who has no particular advantage in the world, reach the goals that he feels are important to him, and by so doing, make a major contribution to others?" His desire to find an answer, coupled with his natural curiosity about the world and its workings, spurred him to become one of the world's foremost experts on success and what makes people successful.

His early career began when, as a member of the Marine Corps, he volunteered to work at a local radio station as an announcer, sharing some of the ideas he had uncovered during his inquisitive youth. The Marines also give him his first chance to travel, although he only got as far as Hawaii when the Japanese attacked Pearl Harbor in 1941. Earl managed to be one of the few survivors aboard the battleship *Arizona*. After five more years in the service, Earl and his wife moved first to Phoenix, then to Chicago, to build what was to be a very fruitful career in network radio. As the host of his own daily commentary program on WGN, Earl arranged a deal that also gave him a commission on his own advertising sales. By 1957, he was so successful he decided to retire at the age of thirty-five.

In the meantime, he had bought his own insurance company and had spent many hours motivating its sales force to greater profits. When he decided to go on vacation for an extended period of time, his sales manager begged him to put his inspirational words on record. The result later became the recording entitled *The Strangest Secret*, the first spoken word message to win a Gold Record by selling over a million copies. About this time, Earl met a successful businessman by the name of Lloyd Conant, and together they began an electronic publishing company that eventually grew to become a multimillion-dollar giant in the self-improvement field. They also developed a syndicated, five-minute, daily radio program, *Our Changing World*, which became the longest-running, most widely syndicated show in radio. Nightingale-Conant Corporation has gone on to publish the audiocassette programs of such well-known authors as Tom Peters, Harvey Mackay, Napoleon Hill, Leo Buscaglia, Denis Waitley, Roger Dawson, Wayne Dyer, Brian Tracy, Tony Robbins, and others too numerous to mention—all leaders in personal and professional development.

When Earl Nightingale died on March 28, 1989, Paul Harvey broke the news to the country on his radio program with the words,

"The sonorous voice of the nightingale was stilled." While he was alive, Earl had found an answer to the question that had inspired him as a youth. He was able to reach valuable goals and, in turn, leave a lasting legacy for others. He had created a life that defines what it means to be "The Essence of Success." In the words of his good friend and commercial announcer Steve King, "Earl Nightingale never let a day go by that he didn't learn something new and, in turn, to pass it on to others. It was his consuming passion."